'IME:
' life
erse

To My Mate Roger!

Best wishes for
the future!

Stee Reed
24/11/94

Marking Country Time

Bygone rural life depicted in words and verse

Steve Reed

PHRAGMITES PUBLISHING LTD.
20 NOTTINGHAM ROAD, BISHOPS CLEEVE,
CHELTENHAM, GLOUCESTERSHIRE, GL52 4BS, UK.

Published in Great Britain 1999 by
PHRAGMITES PUBLISHING LTD.
20 NOTTINGHAM ROAD, BISHOPS CLEEVE,
CHELTENHAM, GLOUCESTERSHIRE, GL52 4BS, UK.

British Library Cataloguing-in-Publication Data.
A catalogue record for this book is available
from the British Library.

ISBN: 0-9536935-0-3

Front cover photograph © Steve Reed:
*"The author's father ploughing
with an iron wheeled standard Fordson, circa 1946."*

Printed by *Manuscript ReSearch Printing*
P.O. Box 33, Bicester, Oxon, OX6 7PP, UK
Tel: 01869 323447/322552   Fax: 01869 324096

CONTENTS

ACKNOWLEDGEMENTS

I would like to recognise the support and encouragement given by the following people.

My mother, for her fund of memories recalled with such clarity. Ian, Grahame, and also Brenda and Janet for contributing photographs. Paul, for constant support and encouragement. Lorna, for spending so many hours typing the original draft and putting the final disk together. My friends, Bob, Jim and Phil, with whom I have enjoyed many a good yarn about old times. Finally, my wife Kate, who suggested the title.

Many others have given support: Phillip, Rachel, Richard, David . . . the list is endless. Thank you to all of you - you know who you are!

INTRODUCTION

I have always considered myself fortunate to have been born and raised in the heart of the English countryside. I feel fortunate also to have lived at a time when rural life moved at a more gentle pace than today.

My memories are of a less intensive method of farming, of smaller fields and of hedgerows brimming with life. The villages of my boyhood were thriving communities, supporting traditional rural businesses. Today, most of those villages have changed and expanded beyond recognition.

The natural span of my life does not permit me to remember all that I have written. I have drawn from the life experience of my parents and from the farm labourers and village people of yesteryear that I have known.

My desire has been to preserve both the memories of myself and others and to impart them to those who care about the countryside and rural life.

Steve Reed
March 1999

A RURAL CHILDHOOD

I was a typical country boy of my time. From an early age, I roamed the fields and local woods, either alone or with my current best friend. We climbed trees, dammed streams, fought and wrestled, and played football on the village green.

Our forays into the surrounding countryside also opened our eyes in no small way to the splendour of Mother Nature. We knew of almost every variety of bird, mammal or fish in the area and everything about them.

At the age of six or seven, I would walk over many fields to find my father at work and even now, on reflection, I believe it was safe enough for me to do so. As soon as I could ride a bicycle, I would go for miles, often up to thirty or forty miles a day during fine weather and so fitness was never a problem! As children, I believe that we used our imagination much more than the youngsters of today. Quite simply, we had to! We did not have the exotic and electronic toys of now. We made things - wooden carts for racing, catapults, stilts, all sorts of things. We played games of marbles and whatever else the season might dictate, because many of our games were dictated by the seasons. If we fell out of sorts with our mates then we fought. Fighting was not frowned upon, bullying was, but not a scrap between two evenly matched lads. You used your fists and fought fair; when the other chap had had enough, he surrendered and that was it, finished. We did get up to mischief, most certainly, but the village policeman was always likely to be around and he definitely influenced our behaviour.

Today it is neither safe nor wise to allow children the freedom that I enjoyed. The pressures of schooling are brought to bear from the earliest of days and the lure of the computer is great. If I have one regret from my childhood, it is that I hated school so much. That was because so many of the teachers could and would, quite legitimately, use force to bring about order. When I look back, I remember so clearly my fear and dread of certain teachers who would not hesitate to beat you for what they considered to be lack of effort. Not unnaturally, I would truant at times when the prospect of double maths could not be endured. I left school at sixteen with no qualifications to my name worth speaking of, yet I knew that I was far from stupid. Today, I firmly believe that education standards are higher than in my day, but I also think that it is much more difficult for teachers to maintain discipline. Somewhere along the way, the balance of control has been lost.

Work came to me well before I left school. Helping on the farm meant long hours in the lambing fields in spring, picking up potatoes, pulling beans, picking fruit and learning to drive a tractor. Along with this came the desire to make money! If there was no work to be had on the farm, then I found other ways of making it. I probably had to work too hard from too early an age, but I was usually keen to do so and it did me little harm. My own children will never work as hard as I did before leaving school, but they will work much harder at school than I ever did - to get on in life, they will have to. Their memories will be so very different from mine, but hopefully they will be as happy.

SCRUMPING

Raiding farmer's orchard
That was so much fun,
But if he saw you at your game
His dog would make you run!

Hiding in the hedgerow
Wait 'til coast is clear,
Always such excitement
Sometimes tinged with fear.

Moving swiftly tree to tree
Flitting like a ghost,
Seeking out the sweetest fruit
Cox it was the most!

Pick the fruit too early
A little pain you'd get!
Never safe to get too far
Away from the toilet!

Hazards there were many
Dog and barbed wire fence,
But at the height of summer
Scrumping would commence!

CAMP FIRES BURNING

Camp fires burning after dark
As cosy as you like,
That was a thing for winter nights
When I was just a tike.

Half-baked spuds cooking in the ashes
Not a good suggestion,
Tasting oh so smoky
Not good for your digestion!

Playing games of make believe
A cowboy on the prairie,
On the watch for rustlers
And other things contrary!

Smoking father's baccy
Feeling slightly sick,
Eyes would sting and start to run
When campfire smoke was thick.

Spitting embers singed your clothes
And hands were nipped by sparks,
Those campfires were lots of fun
So many boyhood larks.

The Hunt sets off (circa 1930)

FOLLOWING THE HUNT

On winter Saturday afternoons
The hunt was out in force,
We used to cycle on behind
And follow up their course.

It really was exciting
To see them in full flow,
And if there was a fox ahead
The hounds would let you know!

I loved to hear the hunting horn
The baying of the hounds,
Carried on the winter wind
They were such mournful sounds.

Those scarlet jackets were a sight
They looked so very grand!
The horses were a thing to see
As they thundered over ground.

We always thought the huntsmen
A bunch of awful snobs,
To us they were a class apart
A lot of snooty nobs!

The fox can be a mighty pest
I know that to my cost,
But it never really bothered me
When his scent the hounds they lost.

RATTING

There always were so many rats
Who made home on the farm,
We'd chase them out with dog and stick
Because they had no charm!

Brown and black and in-between
Some skinny, others fat,
We really didn't want them
That's why we kept a cat!

They lived in barn and in stackyard
And scurried here and there,
They'd sit and stare as if to say
"Catch me if you dare!".

As boys we'd stand with stick in hand
When corn stack it was thrashed,
And when the day was over
We'd count the number we had bashed!

One night I saw a hundred rats
A'moving 'cross the land,
My father said, "Now stand quite still,"
I reached to hold his hand!

They really were a constant pest
And poison they'd not take,
If I never see another
I'll be glad, make no mistake!

THE SUNDAY SCHOOL OUTING

To Sunday school you had to go
No argument or shouting,
But you could always forward look
To the summer Sunday school outing.

Always to the seaside
That you'd always find,
Same place every summer
But you did not mind.

Charabanc it might break down
The journey took forever,
Someone always would be sick
That was none too clever!

Race down to the seafront
The tide is now well in,
Woollen bathing trunks that itch
And chafe against your skin.

Off now to the funfair
Bumper cars of course,
Then on to the roundabout
Ride a wooden horse.

Fish and chips for dinner
Fizzy pop to drink,
What can we do afterwards?
Now let's stop and think!

The hall of magic mirrors
That really was a must,
They made you look so silly
You'd laugh until you bust.

Paddle boats and crazy golf
Digging in the sand,
Plates of jellied eels and whelks
Ice cream in your hand.

As the sun was falling
One last look you'd take,
Then onto the charabanc
Homeward journey you would make.

Tired eyes would droop and close
You'd cuddle up to mother,
That special day it was all done
But next year there'd be another!

KHAKI SHIRTS AND BAGGY SHORTS

Baden Powell the movement started
To raise a better man,
Learn to serve both king and country
That was his noble plan.

Khaki shirts and baggy shorts
Beret and a woggle!
When I think of how I looked
My mind it starts to boggle!

Playing games of pirates
British bulldog too,
Bob a job at Easter
Learn how to clean a shoe!

Summer camp and singing songs
A boy scout that is you,
Something to be proud of
To the movement be so true!

I never was a scout for long
Because I felt a twit,
I wanted to be a timber wolf
But not in patrol peewit!

The boy scouts are a different kind
No longer are out dated,
They wear long trousers now today
Not the baggy shorts I hated!

STICKS AND PINS AND BITS OF STRING

In summertime there often was
A craze to do some fishing,
Sat on riverbank for hours
For the big one you'd be wishing!

Fishing rods that were so crude
Fashioned from all sorts,
Sticks and string and old bent pins
And floats of bottle corks.

Roach were always easy
So were little eels,
Cast your bait of bread or worms
No need for fancy reels.

Sometimes when fish they did not bite
We'd do other things than that,
Like climbing trees and playing chase
With lumps of dried cow pat!

We never really caught that much
But had a lot of fun,
And would always be content
When homeward bound we'd run.

THE VILLAGE CHRISTMAS PARTY

The village Christmas party
Was always so much fun,
You'd have a wash and get dressed up
Then to it you would run.

All your friends and chums were there
The games they would begin,
Musical chairs and postman's knock
On a donkey the tail to pin.

The village reverend keeping order
Such hard work for he!
Peace and order were restored
When it was time for tea.

A gift for every child
And a cracker for to pull,
By the time that tea was finished
Your tummy felt so full.

Frosty air that nips your nose
Hurry home so quick,
Filled to the brim with food and fun
You often felt quite sick!

Up the stairs and off to bed
A time you'd had so hearty,
It always was the season's highlight
The village Christmas party.

POND LIFE

I used to mess about round ponds
When I was just a kid,
And look for all the swimming things
I'll tell you what I did.

I'd look for frog spawn in the spring
To tadpoles it would turn,
I found the way that nature works
And I began to learn.

Crested newts and lizards
Sticklebacks as well,
I'd put them in a jam jar
My garden pond to swell.

The little dustman of the pond
I called the water snail,
For he would keep it nice and clean
And never leave a trail!

Minute beetles, tiny frogs,
Grass snakes on the bank,
I took one home for mother
That earned me quite a spank!

I loved to watch the dragonfly
The sunshine on its wings,
Those ponds they were so much alive
So many beautiful things.

Many ponds have disappeared
Those in farmers' fields,
It really is a tragic loss
Reducing nature's yields.

CATAPULTS AND OTHER BOYHOOD THINGS

A catapult was a prize possession
Hand made and not shop-bought,
We used to shoot at birds and things
And that we shouldn't ought.

Collecting birds eggs in the spring
One from every nest,
Today that's quite illegal
And really for the best.

Build a four-wheel buggy
From cast-off bits of wood,
Race it down the nearest hill
As quickly as you could.

Your pocket knife was kept so sharp
It really was a friend,
And like your favoured catapult
It you'd never lend.

Walking round on home-made stilts
Feeling ten feet tall,
If you lost your balance
You'd take a mighty fall.

Trousers ripped on barbed wire fence
Wrestling in the dirt,
Getting home late after dark
No buttons on your shirt!

Electric gadgets we had none
And not so many toys,
We were a bunch of country lads
A rowdy gang of boys.

FOOTBALL ON THE VILLAGE GREEN

Football on the village green
Played by village boys,
Five-a-side or maybe more
No tactics you'd deploy.

Jackets piled onto the ground
Goalposts for the making,
Games were often played all day
Until your legs were shaking.

Old-fashioned leather-case ball
With stitches often split,
If you tried to head for goal
It would hurt a bit.

No referee nor offside law
The rules they were not many,
You never saw a sending off
And bookings there weren't any.

Shins were always bruised and sore
Trousers sometimes ripped,
And fighting often happened
When you had been tripped!

Goals were scored with frequent ease
Goalkeeper got the blame,
Friendships made and broken
What a lovely game!

A COUNTRY CHILDHOOD

A country childhood in my day
Allowed you so much freedom,
The fields and woods were my domain
Indeed they were my kingdom!

Climbing trees and making camp
Dam or bridge a stream,
Watching rabbits at their play
Hear the vixen scream.

Summertime and out all day
Off to who knows where,
Pretending I was Davy Crockett
Tracking down a bear!

In Autumn time we played at conkers
And built a Guy Fawkes' fire,
When you heard the church clock strike
To home you would retire.

Winter days brought lots of fun
Building igloos in the snow,
I thought to spend the night inside
But to my bed mother made me go!

It isn't quite the same today
More dangers to beware,
Children cannot roam so free
We have to take more care.

EARNING A SHILLING

A shilling I was keen to earn
When I was but a boy,
Could always find a job to do
And payment gave me joy.

Windfall apples by the pound
I sold them door to door,
A man once said as he paid my price
"My boy, you'll never be poor!".

Kindling wood I'd chop for hours
Then load it in a cart,
I knew the folk who'd want to buy
So up the road I'd start.

Bulrushes from the dykes
And mushrooms from the field,
I sold them all where e'er I could
And silver they did yield.

I loved to earn a shilling
That much you'll know by now,
But it wasn't all that easy
I had to work and how!

Bulrushes were much sought after by tourists
and were a good source of pocket money.

VILLAGE LIFE RECALLED

Not so many years ago, those who dwelt in the village made their living either in it or very close to it. Most villages had sufficient shops and facilities that it was not necessary to go to town to do the weekly shopping; with fewer families owning a motor car, it was more essential for that to be the case. After all, towns were for town folk and the countryman did not like to venture too far.

In the village that I lived in, we had a butcher's shop, two grocery stores and a post office. Within near neighbouring villages, there were two bakeries, ironmongers, and I can recall three different blacksmiths' shops, such was the volume of work available - and this long after horses had been replaced on the farms.

If you did not possess a car, the village shop would deliver your weekly order. When I was small, a tradesman would call most days. The baker came three days a week, the grocer once, as did the butcher and fishman. I remember well the butcher's delivery man. Known as 'Old Wicky', he was close to eighty years old but as fit as a fiddle. An old soldier, he was a short dapper man, with a waxed moustache which intrigued me no end. Old Wicky used to enthral me with stories of his days in Kitchener's army when Britain ruled the world. I heard tales of the Boer War, and of the desert and the First World War. I suppose Old Wicky was a less doddery version of the 'Dad's Army' character, Corporal Jones.

At some point in the 1960s, the first supermarkets began to appear in our local town. I can remember when in Sainsbury's, one went to each counter in turn, and was served whatever one required. One day, a new store opened called, I think, 'Priceright', where you wheeled a trolley round and were served at a single cash desk. Convenience foods began to appear, fridges and freezers appeared in households; it was the beginning of the end for the village shop. Also during the 1960s, the first signs of expansion of village boundaries began to materialise; not the large building developments of today, but in-fill between existing properties and maybe half a dozen council houses. Families unknown from further afield moved in. It was the start of things to come.

Entertainment was more local in my parents' day. Every Saturday night there would be a village dance in most every village and the young made little secret of their desire to find life's partner. Dances apart, there were whist drives, beetle drives and people walked far more. Very often, going for a walk was the only way a young courting couple might get some privacy!

I have no idea or theory as to whether village life was or was not better in the old days. I do remember that we had burglaries. Young men had too much to drink and fought, and drove cars - when they had them - when drunk. What I can say with certainty is that village life was very different from today.

SCHOOL DAYS

At the time that my parents went to school, secondary education existed by way of the grammar school. If you passed the entrance examination and your parents could afford the fee, you went. If not, you stayed at the village school until you were fourteen, or younger in some cases.

Many of these village schools are still operative today; solidly built in Victorian times, of redbrick and maybe with three or four classrooms. Literacy and numeracy were driven into pupils with an iron will. Discipline was harsh, even barbaric at times. Children were often caned simply for the fact that they were left-handed. It was not acceptable to write with your left hand and so you were 'persuaded' to use your right.

My mother attended five different schools between 1929 and 1938. The shortest distance that she ever had to walk to school was about three miles. There was no school bus or transport systems. One of the schools that mother attended is no longer a school today, though the old bell still hangs. The bell would ring twice - once, and you had ten minutes to get to school; twice and you went in. If late, you got the cane! Pupils who were late would sometimes, if they had it, rub orange peel into their hands, supposedly to dull the biting pain of the cane.

Before she left for school, my mother had a dozen things to do. There was a house cow to be milked, sheep to be seen to; often she would appear at the school gate, legs splattered with mud and cow muck, often very late!

My own village school was the last school which my mother attended. It was a three classroom affair with an air raid shelter constructed of brick and cast iron. One of my teachers had taught my mother; by the time it came to my turn, she was nearing retirement, but had lost none of her legendary 'pupil management' powers. I can see her now, sat at her desk with a woodbine hanging from the corner of her mouth, surveying the class with an icy stare. I lived in fear of that woman! The day she retired I began to believe in God!

Ah yes! School days! Happy times! How they have changed.

A traditional village school, built at the turn of the century.
The ancient bell still summons pupils to their lessons.

THE VILLAGE SCHOOL

Victorian raised and very small
Classrooms three or four,
Built of stone or red brick
With wood or flagstone floor.

Reading, writing, 'rithmetic
Were what was taught back then,
Starting off with board and chalk
Eventually dip-pen.

From age of five 'til fourteen
To the same school you did go,
If you dared to truant
To your house school-board man would go.

A freely-wielded stick or cane
Kept heads bowed to the task,
Ears clipped by a heavy hand
For trouble you'd not ask!

Those village schools still stand today
But different methods rule,
Computers are the thing today
They're education's tool.

THE OLD VILLAGE SWEET SHOP

Bell that rang above the door
Aladdin's cave within,
Little bars of chocolate
And toffees in a tin.

Sixpence in your pocket
Shiny, hard and true,
So many ways to spend it
Lots of things to chew.

Stand and choose with so much care
Options there are many,
Wine gums, sherbets and pear drops
Blackjacks two a penny.

Aniseed and liquorice stick
And chunks of honeycomb,
Gobstoppers that you know will last
Well after you've got home.

Old English Spangles taste so strong
Fisherman's Friend in winter,
Treacle toffee baked so hard
And on it your teeth could splinter.

All those little treats inside
On which to spend your penny,
To mention all the things you'd see
Why, there's just too many!

THE VILLAGE BAKER

A Saturday job I once had
Twas in the baker's shop,
I ate so many pies and cakes
And thought that I would pop!

I loved the smell of baking bread
Crusty and wholemeal,
No additives nor extras
Just bread so good and real.

Pies he made as well as bread
Steak and kidney were the best,
I always thought I could live on those
And disregard the rest.

The ovens they were fuelled by coke
And always were so hot,
Never empty, always full
And trade there was a lot.

People came from all around
To buy that local bread,
For lunch I'd cut a fresh-baked loaf
And butter I would spread!

That shop it has now closed its doors
The ovens are quite cold,
Like many other village stores
For housing it's been sold.

FOOTPRINTS ON A SAWDUST FLOOR

The Butcher's Shop

Footprints on a sawdust floor
Beef hanging by the side
The village butcher all but gone
Swept off by the EU's tide.

The village butcher where I lived
When I was still a boy
Kept his shop so spick and span
It was his pride and joy.

The meat was mostly local
He knew from whence it came,
In Winter time outside the shop
Hung rows of seasonal game.

His sausages were legend
So full of pork and herbs,
To tell about their flavour
I cannot find the verbs!

Generations going back
Owned that butcher's shop,
But, finally, in '98,
They sold their last pork chop.

That little shop stands empty
No meat is sold today,
European regulations
Had to have their say!

THE BARBER'S SHOP

In every village years ago
There was a man who would cut hair,
It usually was his Sunday job
To wheel out his barber's chair.

He had no fancy salon
But used his garden shed,
A very fair price he charged indeed
For every shaven head.

It was a place to meet and chat
For men to tell tall tales,
They sat on seats of orange box
Small boys on upturned pails.

Men and boys trooped to his door
All looking for a trim,
It sometimes looked like he'd used a bowl
And cut around the rim!

Now we go to salons
And pay a whole lot more,
But many was the Sunday
I walked through that old shed door.

THE OLD VILLAGE INN

Such a different place back then
The working man's preserve,
And when landlord's wife she did appear
Good manners you'd observe.

Sawdust on the bar-room floor
Mainly local beer,
Mild and bitter, brown and light
Bottled Guinness was quite dear.

No neon flashing fruit machine
And juke box there was none,
Games of darts and dominoes
Was how they had their fun.

Bar food, snacks or lunches
Those you would not find,
Only beer and spirits served
And men they did not mind.

Quiet conversation
And never any strife,
A place for men to shelter
Away from nagging wife!

The village inn today
Is quite a different place,
Designer beers and cocktails
Of the past there's little trace.

TRADESMEN CALLING

I knew a time when I was young
When tradesmen used to call,
Every day throughout the week
They'd come to sell their all.

The milkman came six days a week
Butcher and baker twice,
And for the service that they gave
You paid an extra price.

Grocer's van was packed so tight
With all that you might need,
Fruit and veg and sundry goods
A useful man indeed!

The washing machine a luxury was
So the laundry van did call,
For sheets and blankets, other things
That for hand washing were too tall.

Other travellers came to visit
Selling toys and clothes,
But they were often very cheap
Not many bought much of those.

A car in every household
And massive superstores,
Means that in this day and age
Few tradesmen knock on doors.

SAVE THE VILLAGE SHOP?

The village shop is in decline
But does it really matter?
When I look back I can recall
It was a place for 'natter'.

It always seemed you never could
Purchase all your needs,
But you could buy fresh local veg
And sometimes flower seeds.

The shop was always shut by five
Too bad if you forgot,
You would have to just make do
With whatever you had got.

But if you lived too far away
And did not have a car,
You could send your order in
They delivered near and far.

The village shop it should be saved
I think it really must,
For supermarkets out of town
I do not really trust.

A VERY ENGLISH VILLAGE

There is a mythical county called Borcetshire. It must be very small, for it lies between Worcestershire and Warwickshire. Birmingham is but a stone's throw away but the county town is Felpersham, where the Bishop Cyril reigns supreme. Within Borcetshire lies Ambridge, a village trapped in a time-warp; a village built around a traditional green. There are picturesque cottages, a traditional inn and, on the edge, hidden from view, a council development of old age pensioners' bungalows.

In the surrounding countryside, most of the folk - the ordinary ones - earn their living from agriculture. The Archer family are predominant and are looked up to, along with the epitome of modern farming, Brian Aldridge. All others struggle to make an existence. The 'haves' address the 'have-nots' by their first names with condescending patronage. The 'have-nots' address the 'haves', always, as 'Mr', 'Mrs', or even 'Sir'. The 'have-nots' know their place and keep to it.

Anyone who does not go to church, or refuses to join in village life, by means of cricket, fete committee, or any other organisation, is looked down upon. Relatives are always dutifully referred to as 'aunt' or 'uncle', with the utmost of respect, as is only proper for your elders and betters. Until very recent times, a squire was in residence; the peasant farmers would tug non-existent forelocks when they addressed him. The last squire died after suffering two major heart attacks; due, it is said, to the demands made upon him by his younger wife, the fair Caroline Bone, herself an aristocrat of long lineage.

Yes, rural England is alive and well and unchanged, somewhere off the M6. I have looked, but I cannot find it. I am not sure if I really want to, for it sounds a dreadful place. But, for anyone who yearns for an insight into old England past, listen to The Archers on BBC Radio 4. There is, indeed, some attempt at realism, but the programme captures so perfectly the image of country life as seen through urban eyes.

Ambridge is a fair representation of village life some thirty years past. Farming practices are up to date, it is true, even down to genetically modified crop production, but the basic standing of life in Ambridge, in terms of social structure, is a bit wide of the mark. It tells me, however, that there are many who still see rural life in a different way to those of us who are born and bred to it.

THE CARRIER MAN

Before the day of transit van
There was the horse-drawn carrier,
Distance is no object now
But then it was a barrier.

In every town and village place
Goods the carrier hauled,
If it needed shifting
He was the man you called.

A parcel from the station
Things heavy from the shops,
Every day he'd journey
Making lots of drops.

If moving house you had to do
But not too far away,
He'd load your things onto his cart
But that would take all day.

Produce to the market
Then pick up in the town,
But if he came home empty
Then he'd be sure to frown.

The natural successor
Was lorry and the van,
But he gave a sterling service
That horse-drawn carrier man.

THE VILLAGE DANCE

Come Saturday night, come rain or shine
To village dance to have a good time,
The local lads from all around
Considered it their courting ground.

Every village had its dance
For boy to meet girl it gave the chance,
A glance so shy and eyes would meet
Introductions made on dancing feet.

The lads dressed in their Sunday suits
Collar and tie and shiny boots,
Local lass dressed in best frock
To her she hoped the boys would flock.

Up on stage the band would play
The songs and music of the day,
Playing with a rhythmic beat
But hardly in Glenn Miller's street.

If for you she saved last dance
To walk her home you had a chance,
Many a marriage was made that way
At the village dance of yesterday.

THE LOCAL PRODUCE SHOW

Rivalry no stronger found
'Twixt competitor and friend,
The local produce show contributed
So richly to the village life blend.

All summer long men would toil
After work for many hours,
Hoeing, feeding, weeding,
Protecting from seasonal showers.

Agonising choice to make
The question of selection,
And the difference that it would make
Was victory or rejection.

The gardeners' wives laboured long
Over cooking stove,
Chutney, jam and pickle,
Their worthiness to prove.

Secret blends and recipes
Favoured plots of ground,
And come the local produce show
The finest ever found!

OLD VILLAGE MEN

I used to see them sat
On village seat 'neath midday sun,
Stiff of joint and rheumy eyed
Thinking back to days when young.

Waxed handlebar moustache
A waistcoat watch and chain,
They'd sit and chew tobacco
The pavement it would stain.

Some had lost an arm or leg
In Flanders Fields far off,
And there were some you knew
Who had consumptive cough.

Old village men still sit today
Reminiscing in the sun,
I guess my turn will come around
When I'm too old for fun.

THE VILLAGE CRICKET TEAM

We had a village cricket team
I speak of years ago,
A more useless bunch you've never seen
And runs would hardly flow!

There were a few who were too old
And some who were too young,
I played myself when I was twelve
It put me on the rung.

Our opening bat, a man called Bob,
Now he could really hit,
But he was so short and very fat
And could not run a bit.

The village blacksmith was a joke
He'd try to play like Gower,
The best thing that he could have done
Was try to use his power!

We had a bowler who was so fast
But could not keep his line,
He sprayed it wide and always short
And batsmen they would dine!

Our wicket keeper liked to pose
And thought himself so hot,
But as you saw the 'byes' mount up
You'd wish for Alan Knott!

The first game that I played in
They brought me on to bowl,
And three were caught out in the deep
Those wickets I guess I stole!

The worst match that I can recall
Eleven all out I swear!
But I was dropped the week before
So little did I care!

It seems so many years ago
And I have now retired,
But my memories of that useless team
They never have expired!

THE CHANGING VILLAGE

Look at the village and how it's changed
Remember how it grew,
There was a time not long ago
When in it all you knew.

A nation of owners we became
And a house for every man,
But where on earth to build them?
Borough councils began to plan.

"Look at all the villages
There's lots of room to spare;
We can build a hundred homes
We'll dot them here and there."

They ripped out all the hedges
Then levelled out the ground,
Houses sprang up overnight
And chaos all around.

A car in every household
Sometimes even two,
Strangers moving out of town
And so the village grew.

Traffic jams are commonplace
It's all beyond belief,
Now we look to build new roads
To bring about relief.

Where will it end, it just goes on
We see it every day,
If we just keep right on building
The village will have gone away.

Thankfully, some villages remain relatively unchanged

LIVING WITH THE SEASONS

To me, each and every season brought the promise of a new adventure. Winter has always been a favourite of mine, from the earliest days. There is much debate over the changing weather pattern and I am sure that the winters of my childhood were much colder than today.

I can recall ponds and streams being frozen sufficiently to bear the weight of children playing games of 'slides'. Snow was always a possibility and when it came I loved to follow the footprints of the fox across the fields. Once, I felt the need to do this with malice aforethought. During a night-time fall of snow, a fox had taken my Muscovy ducks, Peter and Jemima, and I was heartbroken. My father caught me loading his shotgun! Using the flat of his hand for emphasis, he pointed out the error of my ways. I was eleven years old!

I still love the winter today. It is surprising what winter has to offer to the observant traveller; I will often stop my car and get out for ten minutes to clear my head, and to see what Mother Nature is up to. *Somerset Winter* was inspired by one such occasion.

Springtime always seemed to burst to life with a startling suddenness. One minute, the landscape was cold and bare; the next, you were searching out the earliest primroses and discovering that the rooks had returned to their nesting site in the ancient elms behind the church. On the farm, it was a frantic time. The offspring of rams put in with ewes on Bonfire Night started to appear on the first day of April.

From the age of twelve or thirteen, I would take a week's extra holiday from school to help prepare for lambing. This meant hours spent helping the shepherd sort through those ewes that should have been in lamb, and pulling out those that, by absence of an enlarged udder, appeared not to be. We would then, with the aid of a couple of collie dogs, commence to drive each flock along the road to the lambing field. To me, that was something akin to the old time cowboys trailing a herd to Dodge City. Usually the traffic would be very patient and would, perhaps, enjoy the sight of the dogs nervously chivvying the sheep along. I remember one time, however, when a large Mercedes tried to force a path through the flock. The shepherd asked, and then demanded, that the driver be patient. This did not have any effect, and soon he was at it again, hooting and trying to force his way through. That did it! The shepherd brought his crook down with a mighty crash onto the gleaming bonnet of the Mercedes!

When the outraged Mercedes driver attempted to get out of his car, he was confronted by the immediate likelihood of receiving the same punishment as his car! I stood by, feeling slightly fearful, but also knowing a sense of excitement. I knew that the shepherd was not bluffing and that, had the man not seen sense, it could have been very nasty.

Fortunately for all concerned, the driver got back into his car and turned around to find a different route.

Once lambing started, I would be in the field from first light to fall of night. The shepherd was a man of scant education and was notably short of temper, but I enjoyed working with him and strove to earn his praise. I learnt so much from that man - about shepherding, about the countryside and, perhaps one thing less admirable, he taught me how to swear! The first day that I went out with him, he asked me if I could swear. I mumbled that I might, a bit. His reply was along the lines of "Well, I do, and I aint about to stop now, so you'll have to get used to it! You'll find this job will make you swear as much as it does me! And if you want to swear, or smoke, that's alright by me, but make sure no-one else is around when you do!". He was right, the frustrations of lambs dying and ewes rejecting their infants did lead me to curse and swear. I did not smoke in those days, however.

One occasion that I have never forgotten typifies the less than pleasant side of lambing in those days, but there is also a poignant side to the incident. It was a miserable Sunday evening and darkness was gathering. We were engaged in a struggle to extricate twin lambs who were both already dead and in a state of decay within the ewe. It was usually a losing battle when this happened, for we had no injectable antibiotics and the ewe would usually succumb within days. We always tried, but it was an awful job, literally taking the lambs away a piece at a time on occasions. On this particular night, we were both stripped to the waist, cold, filthy and getting ever more dampened by the misty drizzle drifting across the field.

In the distance, the dim lights of the church could be seen, and the voices of the congregation could be heard, uplifted in their praise of the Lord. I shall never forget the anguished exhalation of that wise shepherd, "I wonder who the Lord thinks is doing the best job tonight then? Us, or them psalm singin' bastards over there?". I wonder indeed!

Memory fades and distorts with time, but summer certainly seems to me to have been so much warmer and longer in those days. Setting off with a bottle of orange squash and a packet of sandwiches, we might be gone all day. Cycling many miles to places further afield, we would return home stiff and sore. Saddles were of a crude nature and we did not have the luxury of multi gear options that cycles have today. School summer holidays also meant work. Potato picking, helping with the harvest and whatever else came along.

Returning to school after the summer break meant that autumn was on the way; football, conkers and competitions to see who could build the biggest bonfire. After dark, we might retire to a camp or den that we had made. Sometimes, those dens were quite comfortable affairs, woven from tree branches and maybe lined with an old tarpaulin. There was always a chimney which might, or might not, allow the camp fire smoke to escape. If my digestion is in any way impaired, it is probably due to the many half-baked potatoes that were incinerated in the ashes of those camp fires!

Finally, autumn gave way to winter once again. I often think that I should have spent a lot more time at my studies and, indeed, I should have. But if I had, would I have had so many happy memories?

I think not!

THE JOYS OF SPRING

Blackthorn hedge in fragrant flower
Shiny wet in springtime shower,
Primrose in a woodland glade
A splash of colour in deepest shade.

Plover wheels 'bove fields of corn
Mistle thrush sings in face of storm,
Blackbird sits on nest so tight
Mad march hares they box and fight.

New-born lambs they stand and shiver
Hunting fox stands all a'quiver,
Baby rabbits born down below
Nature's cycle starts to flow.

Hazel, catkin and pussy willow
Windswept clouds that curl and billow,
Red kite hovers high above
The gentle sound of turtle dove.

Squirrel comes out of his dray
Bright of eye in light of day,
Hedgehog leaves his winter bed
Snorts and coughs to clear his head.

Nights are shorter, days are longer
Sun on your face, it feels much stronger,
Spring is here, a brand new start
And wintertime it doth depart.

SPRING FEVER

In springtime we were always busy
At home and on the farm,
Lambing in the open fields
Spring was hardly calm!

In the fields at break of day
Not home til late at night,
Checking on the ewes and lambs
Until the fall of night.

Spring corn for the planting
Early spuds as well,
Chilly winds knifed through you
Chilblains your ears might swell!

Dragging and a'rolling
Out in grassy fields,
The idea was quite simple
It multiplies the yields.

My face it always turned so brown
From wind and sun all day,
And after Easter back at school
They'd say, "You've had a holiday!".

I really did enjoy those days
Though hours were oh so long,
But that hard work it did me good
It helped to make me strong.

THOSE HAZY DAYS OF SUMMER

Those summer days of long ago
They seemed to last forever,
It never seemed to rain at all
We had the best of weather.

The sun it always burned so bright
And never was sky so blue,
But was that really how it was?
Is my memory all that true?

It seemed that you could play all day
No need to wear a jacket,
Going on a cycle ride
Squash and a lunch packet.

The rivers and the little streams
Their water fell so low,
And as you wound your way back home
Your feet would move so slow.

We never seem to have a summer
It seems so wet and cold,
Not like those far off years ago
At least that's what we're told!

FALL BREAKS AND BACK TO WINTER

Glories of Autumn
Are almost gone,
Winter is creeping
The days are less long.

Weak is the sunlight
Strong are the nights,
Howling wind bemoans
Its plight.

Leaves torn asunder
In late Autumn plunder,
Far out to sea
A roll of thunder.

Frost in the morning
Thick fog at night,
Dark heavy clouds
Suppress pale moonlight.

Frozen leaves crackle
Like fire-licked tinder,
Fall breaks
And back to Winter.

FOG

I remember a time
Many years since gone,
I was lost in a fog
For home I did long.

Out in the fields
And on my way home,
The fog rolled in
Like an opaque dome.

The lights on my tractor
Would not pierce the gloom,
At times I thought surely
I would drive to my doom.

I drove through the fields
Not knowing my way,
At one time I even
Began to pray.

The fog was so thick
It swirled and unfurled;
I seemed to be
In a different world.

I looked in vain
For lights at the farm,
By now I was feeling
A sense of alarm!

As I lost hope
A sight I did see,
My faithful old collie
Came looking for me.

I made it at last
Led home by my dog;
I'll never forget
That night in the fog!

PLAYING AFTER DARK

Playing after dark was fun
We'd roam so free and wild,
Sometimes we'd light a fire
If nights were less than mild.

A woodland den at night was snug
Spuds cooked in a smoky pyre,
Laying ambush to our mates
Of that we did not tire!

A derelict house on rainy nights
Became a sailing ship,
One night I hurt myself so bad
As down the stairs did slip.

Knock on doors and run away
And other silly games,
Played the fool and paid the price
And never made the gains!

A COUNTRY CHRISTMAS

Not much time to sit and lounge
The farm did not stand still,
But it was such a special time
Of it ourselves we'd fill.

Tree cut from our own supply
And house bedecked with holly,
Chestnuts roasted on the fire
The time was always jolly.

Off to bed on Christmas eve
Waiting for the day,
Pillowcase at end of bed
New games for us to play!

Cockerel, goose or turkey
Raised out in the yard,
Mother's cooking was so good
To eat it wasn't hard!

The day it always seemed so cold
And fitting for the season,
So much unlike this day and age
When sun shines for no reason!

Boxing day it came and went
And back to work the next day,
For there was little time back then
For folk to stop and play.

WINTER SNOW

I recall a heavy snow fall
Way back in sixty-two,
We were cut off for days on end
That much I swear is true.

The lanes were blocked by mighty drifts
And snow plough never came,
I could not even get to school
But there could be no blame.

The snow it fell then fell again
It was so bitter cold,
The worst snow storm for twenty years
At least that's what I'm told.

Electricity was off for days
There was no telephone,
As kids we really did not mind
For we were snug at home.

My father though he found it tough
To get out to the farm,
The sheep and cows he had to check
To keep them safe from harm.

By firelight we ate our tea
With candles on the go,
Then up the stairs and off to bed
'Gainst window snow would blow.

We woke up in the morning
With ice inside the pane,
And when your bare feet touched the lino
The shock would reach your brain!

Eventually they cleared the drifts
The snow began to melt,
And even I began to cheer
For boredom I had felt.

The village school returned to life
With children it did swell,
One thing for sure that you can bet
A story we could tell!

COLD DAYS IN DECEMBER

When I was a boy
And still very small
In the time of December
The mercury would fall.

Frost on the windows
The ponds they would freeze
But once I remember
Christmas snow on the trees.

A sudden sharp snap
Is all that we get
Sunshine at Christmas
More usually wet.

Cold days in December
Now seem oh so rare
December now seems
A month mild and fair.

SOMERSET WINTER

I went down to Cheddar
On a chill Winter's day.
A cold, barren landscape
It seemed that way.

I stopped my car
And got out to rest,
The air was so clean
I felt so refreshed.

Gorse-strewn pastures
Some littered with stone;
Thin, hungry meadows
Grazed down to the bone.

Poor ragged sheep
And hunched, scrawny cows;
Small stunted trees
With short twisted boughs.

Rooks by the score
Making raucous chatter;
Like black-gowned old ladies
Having a natter!

Replenished at last
I returned to my task.
I'd seen more than I thought
What more could I ask?

BARE FIELDS IN WINTER

Stand at the edge
What do you see?
More than you'd think
Believe you me!

Cock pheasant strutting
Displaying his wares;
Brown hare frolics
And has no cares.

Faded old stubble
Dusted with frost;
Hunting hawk swoops
Field mouse is lost!

Stand very still
You may well see
Sly fox prowling
Along the lea.

Roe deer at dawn
Can sometimes be seen;
Don't make a move!
Their senses are keen.

Little owl hunts
By day and by night;
Rests on a gate
In broad sunlight.

Bare fields in Winter
May not be so empty;
Look hard and you'll see
Interest a'plenty!

At work in the rearing pens.
Eggs collected from pheasant nests were placed under broody hens.

HEROES AND VILLAINS

In conversation about 'the old days', anecdotes are invariably told about certain characters, the like of whom are not met today. It may be that the work that gave them their living has disappeared, or that society no longer finds them acceptable or indeed that they have been replaced and upgraded.

The local poacher and molecatcher are two of a kind that I remember well; often their role in country society overlapped. Both would have had great knowledge of wildlife and, while sometimes the poacher was a source of irritation, providing he was what was known as a 'one for the pot' man, he might be tolerated - but both gamekeeper and village policeman would let him know that they had their eye on him.

The molecatcher would not be above a little skulduggery himself. If he were too successful at clearing moles, he might be out of work!

The village policeman was either loved or hated; as small boys we tended to be very wary of him. He always seemed to be examining our faces for signs of guilt and, indeed, because we never knew when he was going to appear, we did tend not to take too many chances if the thought of mischief crossed our minds.

It is rare today to see a rural tramp but, when I was a boy, we used to see them a lot. Very unkempt, bearded, dressed in layers of cast-off clothes and always hungry, they would call door to door hoping for a food parcel or a drink. Very often they would not speak but would just stand in hope or expectation. My mother rarely turned them away and would give them a doorstep of bread smeared with butter, and a hunk of cheese. If it was proffered, she would refill their water bottle. Because of their appearance, which could be quite alarming, many were nervous of them, but they did not usually cause any trouble.

There was a blacksmith in nearly every village that I knew. Apart from shoeing horses, they fashioned tools and repaired farm implements. They were, through necessity, a powerfully-built breed and a visit to the forge to see what they were working at was a regular occurrence. Our own village smith would smote the cricket ball many a mile on Friday night practice, but come Saturday he would try to play like David Gower, elegantly stroking the ball rather than clubbing it. He was usually out for a very low score!

Gypsies would often camp in the lanes around and about. They might do casual farm work such as pulling beans or picking up potatoes. Their ragged children would sometimes come to school but would often sleep through the lessons. I was always wary of passing their camps because of their fierce dogs and because of the mythology surrounding them.

The council roadman was the butt of many a joke. It was always said that if you took his broom away he would fall down! He was always to be seen, sweeping, mending or trimming the roadside verge.

There was a type of chap who never settled to a regular job but worked to a regular system, working through the casual season as a fruit or potato picker then perhaps doing some hedging or ditching. He would then sign on to the dole for a few months until work came again. As the work that he did was piece rate paid, the harder he worked the more he earned. One that I knew always had the latest model of Ford Cortina and spent Christmas in a good hotel!

The tinker could be a right pest! Very persistent and always calling to sharpen knives or to beg scrap metal, for which he might pay a few shillings. He was often of the gypsy type but was not a true Romany.

The old-time gamekeeper had a different way of working. That is not to say that keepering is an easy job today - it is far from that. But with ready-mixed game feed and medication to keep bird losses to a minimum, it is a different job today. The demands are still for a man who knows the countryside and, at the end of the day, produces good sport for the guns.

Many of these men were, indeed, 'characters', eccentric of nature and sometimes just plain cantankerous, but they added a certain colour to their surroundings.

THE OLD GAMEKEEPER

The keeper's days were long and hard
It was a lonely life,
Many hours spent out of doors
Away from kids and wife.

Raising broods of pheasant
And maybe partridge too,
That was not an easy job
I'll give you just a clue.

Eggs taken from a hidden nest
And put 'neath a broody hen,
They spent their early days of life
Cooped up in rearing pen.

The game food it was mixed by hand
For it you could not buy,
That's not a job they'd do today
They wouldn't even try.

Boiled rabbit and biscuit meal
Mixed with eggs and rice,
The blend it had to be just right
Or birds died in a trice.

Vermin were a problem
Sparrowhawk or jay,
Their number had to be kept down
For on pheasant chick they'd prey.

The poacher too he was about
Especially late at night,
He often was a desperate man
And he would stand and fight.

When the gentry came to shoot
Upon a winter's day,
That was the keeper's time of test
Had he earned his pay?

Pheasant shoots there are today
And keeper he still rules,
But his job has altered now
He has some different tools.

Dressed in his working clothes.
The old gamekeeper (circa 1930)

A POACHING MAN

My father was a poaching man
And knew a trick or two,
With gun or snare he had no match
His aim was good and true.

A rabbit or a pheasant
Trout or maybe duck,
Nothing was a problem
That was skill not luck.

Ferret down a rabbit's burrow
Panic deep below,
Rabbit shoots out of his bolt hole
Poacher can't be slow!

Beer soaked corn on woodland path
Pheasant for to feed,
When pheasant gets a little drunk
He's easy prey indeed!

Tickled trout needs speed of hand
Patience and keen eye,
Moonlit night brought flocks of duck
To mill pond they would fly.

Many was the countryman
Who kept his family fed,
By going poaching late at night
While others were a'bed.

Poaching still goes on today
But in a different way,
Often by large gangs of men
Who want to make it pay.

My father. A poaching man!

THE VILLAGE BOBBY

The village bobby I recall
He was never far away,
And petty crime was so much less
Because it did not pay.

He always knew the local rogues
And kept them on their toes,
You'd always see him day and night
When he rested heaven knows.

As country lads we loved to roam
And sometimes did some wrong,
We knew that if we went too far
He'd catch up before so long.

Policing today is a different thing
The village bobby's gone,
I really think he should return
And hope it won't be long!

A DIFFERENT BREED

I used to see the gypsy camps
They'd come throughout the year,
And if I had to pass them by
I'd feel a little fear.

Their Romany faces looked so foreign
They seemed a breed apart,
No sooner had they set up camp
The police made them depart.

Sometimes they seemed to find a place
Where they could stop in peace;
I knew a shepherd who lost a sheep
But then he saw its fleece!

They often were accused of theft
Sometimes I'm sure they did,
Would they steal me? I would think
But I was just a kid.

Their children sometimes came to school
But couldn't read or write,
If you called them names at break
There'd always be a fight!

New age travellers you will see
Much more than gypsy camp,
But they are something else again
Quite a different stamp.

THE VILLAGE SMITH

Thirty years ago or more
I remember the blacksmith well,
His furnace always burned so bright
Just like the fires of hell.

My father had his garden tools
Designed and made by hand,
Hammered in the local forge
The test of time they'll stand.

I used to go down to the smith
To see the horses shod,
The blacksmith was a mighty man
To me he was a god.

The forge it was a busy place
For it there was a need,
Mending this and making that
A vital source indeed.

Village forges still remain
Their work is not the same,
Ornamental this and that
It's quite a different game.

THE GENTLEMEN OF THE ROAD

I used to see when I was young
The gentlemen of the road,
Tramps and beggars they were called
But they lived to a certain code.

They used to call upon our house
Never asking for very much,
A hunk of bread, a chunk of cheese
And always pleased for such.

I used to ask from whence they'd come
Mother would say she'd heard,
That many returning from the war
Had not rejoined the herd.

Worldly goods tied up in bundles
Wheeled sometimes on a cart,
Always ragged and unshaven
They were a breed apart.

In Autumn time when they came
They'd beg for warmer clothes,
But I never saw a tramp in Winter
Where they went, only heaven knows.

A country tramp is rare today
They've all but gone away,
They are of different ilk now
And in the towns they stay.

THE COUNCIL ROADMAN

Country roads of years ago
Were serviced to a plan,
Verges, lanes and by-ways
The preserve of the council man.

The council roadman worked his patch
Filling hole and rut,
And when the verge was overgrown
With scythe the grass he'd cut.

He never seemed that busy
Was always brewing tea,
And if I ever passed him by
He'd stop and talk to me.

Always dressed in corduroy
Cloth cap on his head,
If you took his broom away
Down he'd fall twas said!

The local roadman is no more
His day came to an end,
Pensioned off, redundant made
No more the roads to mend.

A TINKER'S CUSS

A tinker man called Sammy
Used to call around,
He'd ask for pots and pans to mend
And try to charge a pound!

He drove a rusty lorry
Filled with old scrap metal,
Keen to buy whate'er you had
But on price so slow to settle!

Knotted scarf around his neck
A greasy trilby on his head,
His clothes were always dirty
But he always looked well fed.

He'd ask to sharpen knives and things
"I won't charge you a lot",
But when you got them back again
Could they cut? Oh no, how they
would not!

When to his ways you grew so wise
And said, *"Thank you, not today,"*
He'd swear and cuss an awful lot
Then stand and hope you'd sway!

No-one really liked him
Trustworthy he was not,
You'd never get an honest deal
From him you'd surely not!

THE CASUAL WAY

There was a breed of men I knew
Who worked a casual way,
They'd pick potatoes or clear a ditch
For piece-work rates of pay.

Seasonal work on farms there was
For men of varied skill,
They could make enough to live
If they worked hard with a will.

Pulling beans and picking fruit
Harvest help as well,
The work it might not last for long
And that you could never tell.

In winter months there was no work
And so they went on to the dole,
But by working hard in summer time
They'd bought their winter coal!

Income tax they did not know
They lived in council houses,
Such a casual breed of men
But they kept their kids and spouses!

THE VILLAGE GOSSIP

There was a woman near to us
Who loved to probe and pry,
She always asked what you were doing
And then she'd ask you why!

Known as the village busy body
She knew your every move,
And always loved a right old gossip
Her knowledge just to prove!

We loved to cheek and tease her
And tell outrageous lies,
Like saying we were orphans
And us she did despise!

One day she learned her lesson
For our story, how she fell!
About the vicar's love affair
And off she went to tell!

The vicar he was not amused
In fact he lost his calm,
And when he saw her after church
He sang a right old psalm!

Eventually she moved away
With relief the village sighed,
But I often felt a sense of guilt
About the times I lied!

'DICK THE CATCHER'

I knew a man many years ago
The local mole catcher was he,
If farmers' fields were over run
He'd clear them for a fee.

With terrier dog at his heel
He'd set his many traps,
If I saw him I would ask, "Any luck?"
He'd only answer, "P'raps".

Known to all as 'Dick the Catcher'
He lived and worked alone,
Always very short on words
But never known to moan.

When to the village people moved
He'd visit late at night,
And in the morning when they looked
Their garden was a sight!

Little mounds of earth appeared
Laid by Dick's own hand,
Then the offer would be made
"Of moles I'll clear your land"!

Dick the Catcher is no more
His time came to an end,
Of his ilk we'll no more see
On that you can depend!

BYGONE FARMING WAYS

When I was a boy, farms employed many more labourers than today. There were the skilled tractor drivers for ploughing and field work, but there was always a place for a relatively unskilled chap, providing that he was fit and strong.

The tractors of those days did not have the massive horsepower of today, nor did they offer the comfort of air conditioned, sound-proofed cabs. I can well recall my father swathed in layers of clothing, topped off with an army greatcoat, to combat the freezing winds when ploughing with an old lend-lease vintage caterpillar crawler.

I've heard it often said that it must have been 'better' when ploughing was done by horses. Ask anyone who remembers those days and they will tell you that it was hard on man and beast. Farm labourers were old men well before retirement; working long hours in all weather meant that rheumatism was common place. Corn was bagged in hessian sacks weighing two and a quarter hundred weight and these would be carried on backs that eventually would give way.

Today, it is not uncommon for farm workers to own their house, although the traditional tied cottage is still preferred by many. Usually the farm-worker's cottage is of modern design or, if not, has seen thorough renovation over the years. It is accepted that if the highest quality workmen are required then the highest quality package must be on offer. If the cottage available is of a poor standard, then it follows today that a farm worker worth his salt will decline to live in less than acceptable conditions.

It was not always this way. The cottage into which I was born did not have hot running water until I was seven and I can still recall the old tin bath tub on the kitchen floor! If the farm workers cottage required maintenance, one might have to put up with a leaking roof, as there was no automatic right to a certain standard. I knew of one who waited until the start of lambing before handing in his notice, because he was sick and tired of, as he put it, "lying a'bed at night and watching the stars go by!". His resignation was refused and within a week he had been moved to a superior house, while his was razed to the ground and totally rebuilt! It took such extreme action at such a critical time of the farming year to achieve what had been requested so many times before.

A farm worker is protected by the same codes of practice that apply to any other industry. Health and safety inspections are made and working conditions must conform to a standard. My mother can clearly recall seeing families wheeling their possessions on a hand cart, having been removed from their tied cottage by bailiffs, probably for a minor misdemeanour. A minute's notice might be given on the flimsiest of reasons, and there was little or no protection. My own grandfather took the unusual step of appealing to his union when dismissed unjustly. His case was proven and he was awarded fifteen pounds compensation!

The idyllic picture often painted of farm life is frequently misleading. Farms are so much bigger today. The tractors and ploughs are bigger and so are the yields. The labour force is much, much smaller. Wages are more realistic and the traditional tied cottage is more usually modern and well-maintained.

I am not sure that many of today's farm workers would willingly exchange their life today with their counterparts of yesterday.

A Massey Harris 'Bagger' combine, circa 1955.
How unlike the air conditioned juggernauts of today!

A FARM LABOURER'S LOT

A farm labourer's life was very hard
Such long hours and endless toil,
Most everything was done by hand
And labourers' health did spoil.

Corn was carried in heavy sacks
That weighed two hundred weight and more,
Hauled 'cross yards and up granary stairs
And backs were stiff and sore.

Ploughing was done by man and horse
A most idyllic scene,
But in winter months when mud was thick
Horse was wreathed in steam.

Crops were hoed and pulled by hand
Come snow, sunshine or rain,
Rheumatism froze their joints
And men they worked in pain.

Holidays they did not have
And pay was very poor,
If a man got sick and bad
He could lose his job for sure.

Men got old before their time
And pensions there were none;
Life it was so very hard
With little time for fun.

YESTERDAY'S HARVEST

The harvest is gathered oh so fast
In this day and age,
It wasn't always done this way
So let's turn back a page.

Even in my grandpa's day
Corn was cut by hand,
Men with scythes they worked so hard
With little time to stand.

Sheaves were tied and then were stooked
Carried home by horse and waggon,
Midday lunch was bread and cheese
With cider from a flagon.

Rabbits would run for cover
As the corn was cut,
Gangs of boys would chase them out
With sticks of hazel nut.

The sheaves were stacked and then were
thatched
Against inclement weather,
The work was done by doughty men
Whose skin was tanned like leather.

When the corn was sold the thrasher came
Separating wheat from chaff,
Terrier dogs they fought with rats
And men would stand and laugh.

Combine harvester rules today
The fields of wheat they plunder,
Moving at a rapid pace
The crop is torn asunder.

Harvest is an easier task
It needs a lot less men,
There are still a few who knew it different
In the days of way back then.

The author's father.
Another load of sheaves brought safely in.

ODE TO THE STACK THATCHER

My father, Ronald Reed, was one of the last men on Romney Marsh to continue thatching his hay and straw stacks. He was also one of the very best exponents of that ancient craft. People have told me that a stack thatched by Ron Reed would keep the wet at bay more effectively than any tarpaulin.

Thatching up to fifty stacks a year, from the earliest hay in June to late wheat in September, father would start work at first light to get as much done as possible. If the breeze became too stiff, the job became difficult if not impossible.

The bain of father's life was a badly finished stack where the Norfolk reed could not easily be packed into place, followed closely by reed that had been cut too short.

I remember so clearly my job as 'thatcher's mate'. It would be my task to haul reed bundles and stumps up the ladder and to make sure the billy was always boiling for tea. Father finally stopped thatching around 1968.

The author's father at work, circa 1960.

STACK THATCHING MAN

Build the stack with skill and care
Keep it nice and tight!
Terraced layers at the top
Thatcher needs it right.

Cut the reeds and let them dry
Make sure that they are long,
If they're not it makes it hard
Thatcher sings a song!

Thatchers prayer last thing at night
"No wind tomorrow, please!
For if there is, I know for sure,
The reed the breeze will tease."

Start out at the crack of dawn
Early is the hour,
Who knows what lies ahead today
Stiff wind, a storm or shower.

Tools laid out all set to go
Billy on the boil,
Thatching is a thirsty job
It is a ceaseless toil.

Take the reed and pack it tight
Fill in all the gaps,
String it down and hold it firm
Make sure it overlaps!

Neighbouring farmer stops to look
Admires the job out loud,
"You've done a damn fine job of that!"
Thatcher feels so proud.

Stack thatching was a skillful craft
It had to be done well,
If thatcher did a shoddy job
By Winter you could tell!

The finished article.
Once a familiar sight, but not for the last thirty years.

HORSEPOWER DAYS

Smokey fumes of paraffin
Always slow to start,
Tractor came onto the land
Horse it did depart.

Waggoner did bemoan his loss
Progress - what is that?
Tractor has no character
To it you cannot chat.

A fine old picture, horse and plough,
But hard on man and beast;
Tractor never feels the pain
It's kinder now at least.

As years went by
Their strength and power grew,
Little fields they disappeared
Dykes and hedges too.

Fewer men were needed
To turn and work the ground,
Landscapes changed forever
Not for the best I've found.

Tradition is a wonderful thing
There are those who progress grudge,
Was it better then or now?
Who can really judge?

Ploughing at Stonesfield, near Witney in Oxfordshire, circa 1938.

A WAGGONER'S TALE

Tractor driver rules today
On the farm he's king,
The waggoner came before him
His story I will bring.

Up at early hour
Long before the rest,
Get the horses ready
Got to look their best.

Feed them well with oats and hay
Make sure that they are fit,
Ploughing heavy land today
It's sure to hurt a bit.

Mud that sucks and clings so tight
The going's really slow,
If only this were lighter ground
Then I'd really flow.

Plod our weary way back home
The moon is rising fast,
Not many acres done today
The boss will damn and blast!

Back into the stable
Light the lamp to see,
Never home so early
Always late for tea.

Summer time I'm up by four
The daylight comes too early,
There's got to be a better way
I know there must be surely?

Hay and corn must be brought in
The barns they must be filled,
To work so many hours
Man and horse must be strong-willed.

Hauling logs down to the mill
Walking at the head,
It really is too many miles
My feet they feel like lead.

Tractor drivers of today
You've really got it made!
Your metal steed it moves so fast
And you're even quite well paid!

An early standard Fordson tractor, the introduction of which
signalled the beginning of the end for horse power.

DIFFERENT DAYS, DIFFERENT WAYS

Farming today is a different job
So many changes we see,
I can remember a different time and place
It was better that way to me.

Work was done in other ways
And different tools were used,
The land was treated fairly
And never was abused.

The fields they were much smaller
And hedges there were many,
Wild life in great abundance
And work for all a'plenty.

Machinery got much bigger
Production pressure grew,
Food for all was needed
That much I know is true.

Trees and hedges disappeared
The land became a prairie,
It might have made a difference
To me it was contrary.

Chemicals and pesticides
Have raised and increased yield,
But where has all the flavour gone
In produce from the field?

Less labour is needed here today
And subsidy it rules.
Are we that much better off?
Or are we all just fools?

Back breaking work!

112

POTATO PICKING DAYS

Potatoes used to be picked by hand
By gangs of workers upon the land.
The work was hard but it paid well
I've done it myself, my coffers to swell.

The bine it was topped by a flailing thing
And through the air the debris would sing;
Followed behind by a tractor and spinner
Farmer could tell if his crop was a winner.

Pickers worked in a bent or stooped way
As fast as they could to boost their pay;
The sun when it got hot made the job very tough
If the tractor broke down the language got rough.

The bigger the tater the lower the pay
We worked in all weather, come what may;
The smaller the spud the more money we got
First crop of earlys were best of the lot.

The green and the split were left on the ground
But not always so if the boss wasn't around!
If your back it ached and you got somewhat slow
You held up the job, they'd sure let you know!

Done now by machine, fields cleared in a day
It wasn't so long that it wasn't that way.
Potato picking the bones it did hurt
But pound notes a'plenty there were in the dirt!

CLAMPING AND RIDDLING

Once potatoes had been lifted, they were carried to the edge of the field and clamped. Clamping was like building a stack; it had to be done correctly or the crop could perish.

The clamper was a man with recognised skill and it was his job to lay the potatoes and to make the final covering as weatherproof as possible. First, the size of the clamp would be calculated. The base would then be dug out to about a spade's depth. The spits of earth were put to one side and a layer of straw was placed on the ground to cover the base of the clamp; this would give protection against ground frost. Then came the potatoes. They were carefully laid in layers, care being taken to avoid bruising or damage to the skins. Each layer got progressively smaller so that the end result was a clamp with sloping sides that would allow the rain to run off. Finally, the covering was applied. Dependent upon which part of the country you were in, this would be either straw or Norfolk reed. Laid to a depth of two or three feet, the reed or straw would then be covered in turn with the spits of earth removed from the base. Care had to be taken to leave a narrow gap along the ridge to allow the clamp to breathe. Sometimes, clay drainage pipe with holes in would be strategically laid upright in the clamp to aid breathing.

When it was time for the potatoes to be sold, a motor driven riddle would be hauled down to the field. The clamp would be uncovered and the potatoes shovelled onto the slow moving conveyor. There would be three or four men or women 'picking off', looking for potatoes that were green, bad or unsuitable for sale. These were discarded and might be used for feeding to sheep or pigs. Those that were good trundled down the conveyor into hessian sacks, attached at the end, and then were carried away.

Potato riddling had to be done in a thorough way or complaints would be made by the purchaser, but it was a dull, boring job, done in the open and often in freezing cold weather. Other crops such as turnips, beet and mangolds were also clamped for protection against the elements.

Clamping and riddling
Circa 1946
The riddle is a hand turned model

MARKET DAY

Pigs and sheep went off each week
Down to the local market,
Cows as well and other things
Like rabbits in a basket.

Farmer's wife would dress her best
To do a little shopping,
Farmer always hoped and prayed
That prices were not dropping.

The auctioneer he plied his trade
His voice a mighty holler,
He spoke at such a rapid pace
It was so hard to follow.

Idle men would stand around
Admiring pens of stock,
When time for lunch it came around
To market café they'd flock.

You could buy and sell most anything
From corn to local fruits,
A horse or plough, a milking cow,
And brand new working boots.

It was a weekly outing
For farmer and his wife,
A trip to town on market day
Twas part of farming life.

THISTLES IN THE FARMER'S FIELD

A thistle you will hardly see
In pastures now today,
They're sprayed and die before they're grown
I suppose it's better that way?

Before this age of chemicals
There was another way,
So just read on and I will tell
Of another far off day.

Dug out with a thistle spud
Long-handled, with a blade,
It was the work of women
And they were poorly paid.

Digging in the midday sun
Walking up and down,
And if you dared to miss one
The foreman he would frown.

Thistles in a pasture
Not good for cow or sheep,
You did not want them in your hay
No good for winter keep.

I suppose there was a bonus
For on them life did feed,
Goldfinches by the dozen
Would peck out all the seed.

A thistle you will hardly see
They really cannot stay,
But spraying off with poison?
Not really nature's way.

A GOOD SHEPHERD

An ancient shepherd that I knew
Turned eighty-five and more,
Has knowledge that cannot be bought
His mind's a massive store.

He's spent his life out on the land
Trained at his father's heel,
Left school at an early age
But his instinct is so real.

Life that's been spent in the open fields
His skin so tanned like leather,
From years of wind and sun and rain
And all kinds of inclement weather.

Eighty hours a week and more
Throughout the lambing time,
Crack of dawn til late at night
And for his bed he'd pine.

He learnt to shear and dag by hand
So many years ago,
His hands were sore and back did ache
And sweat on his brow would glow.

Always working on his own
Except for collie dog,
Each day he'd walk for many miles
At a steady rhythmic slog.

Now he is so very old
His legs are far from steady,
But his mind is razor sharp
And still for work he's ready!

Younger shepherds seek him out
His help they still require,
I asked him once, "When will you stop?"
He said, "I'll die when I retire!".

The author's uncle — George Elvy
Shearing by hand, circa 1948.

And today, aged 82,
still sought for his experience and advice.

THE FARM LABOURER'S COTTAGE

Part of a tradition
That hasn't gone away,
Now often very modern
But not in father's day.

Sometimes very isolated
And miles from anywhere,
Not in good condition
And farmer did not care.

Running water there was none
Twas pumped up from a well,
Always very low in summer
If rain it had not fell.

No electric light bulb
Nor gas lamp in his day,
They had to light an oil lamp
At the end of day.

There was no indoor plumbing
Not of any kind,
At the garden end
An earth closet you would find!

Cooking on a coal-fired stove
No central heated room,
When it came to housework
You swept up with a broom.

Bath night only once a week
Tin tub on the hearth,
Water used by one and all
What a way to bath!

Roses round the cottage door
Idyllic country scene,
But if you took a look inside
For it you would not dream!

THE COUNTRYSIDE AT WAR

Although born twelve years after the conclusion of the Second World War, as a young boy growing up in the sixties I loved to listen to my parents' memories of having lived and worked on the land during that time.

Living in the south east corner of Kent, they experienced the Battle of Britain at first hand. Dogfights raged overhead and, down below, they prepared for invasion. It was not so much a case of 'if' but 'when'! The church bells were silent, to be rung only when invasion happened; and the signposts were all removed.

Farming carried on as best it could. When the battle up above was at its peak, that sometimes became difficult. My mother, on one boiling hot day, took all morning to move a flock of sheep a relatively short distance. At one point she recalls lying flat on the ground, while the fight came down to tree-top level and bullets tore up the grass around her. When it was over, she discovered that she had been gripping hold of two thistles and never felt the pain!

My father worked on the farm by day and, in the evening, donned his home guard uniform. The local troop would go on coastal watch and stand guard on strategic points. My Uncle George was doing something a little different. He, too, worked on the land by day, but had the invasion happened he would have taken his part in what was then a most secret organisation, known simply as the auxiliary units. In fact, these auxiliary units would have formed the backbone of the resistance movement following invasion. Trained secretly to handle explosives and in the art of silent killing, they would have operated from bunkers of which the remaining ones are still not all known today. It is only in the last ten years that my uncle's part in this organisation became known. His parents never knew and he himself modestly says that it did not seem that important.

Farming really began to change during the war. Previously bread wheat was not grown and so much food and raw materials were imported from the commonwealth countries. Tractors began to appear, although the horse still ruled. I can remember my father driving a D2 caterpillar crawler in the 1960s that had come from America during the war as part of the lease-lend agreement.

The Women's Land Army needs little introduction, but such a vital role they played. Prisoners of war were also made to help on the land and many stayed after the end of the war. At my village school, there were several children whose fathers were ex-POWs.

Over the years, I have talked to many people who lived and worked in the countryside during those desperate years and their memories must be preserved as they grow rapidly old.

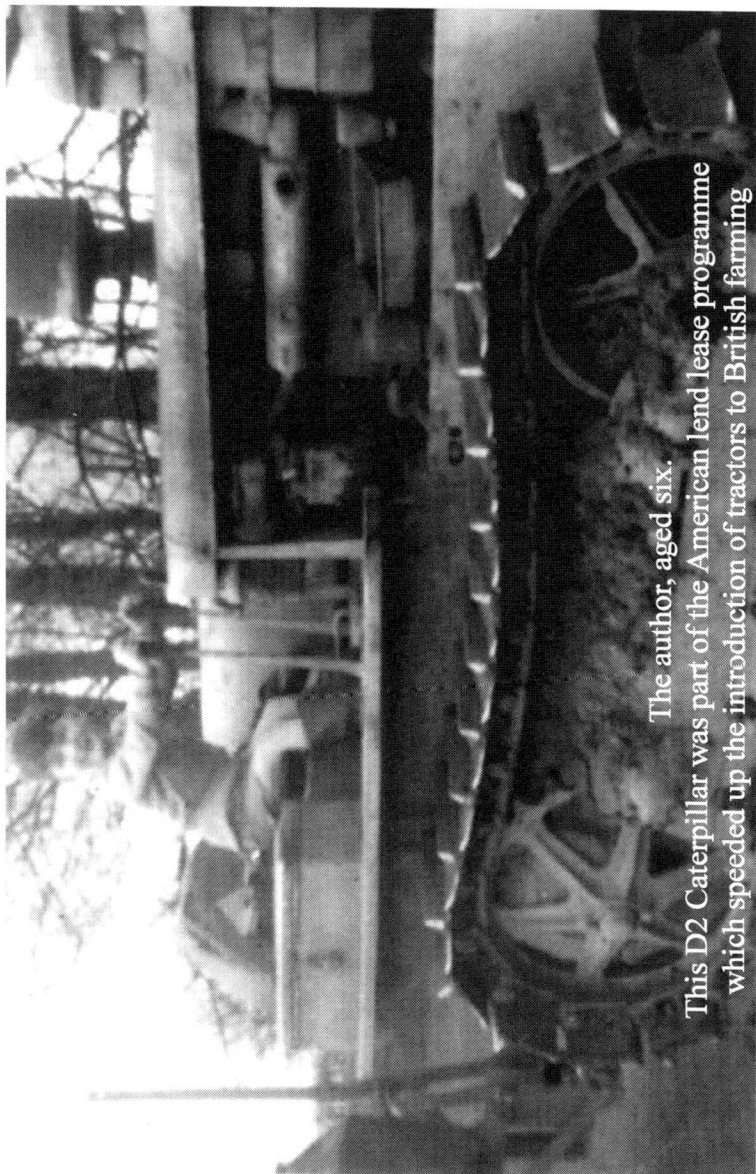

The author, aged six.
This D2 Caterpillar was part of the American lend lease programme which speeded up the introduction of tractors to British farming

WHEN INVASION THREATENED

They took down all the signposts
Confusion for to cause,
If Nazi troops had landed
At crossroads they might pause!

The village church its bells were still
For invasion they would ring,
And if you heard that sound peal out
Panic it would bring!

Pill box structures did appear
At vital turn of road,
Twas hoped that things might be held up
Invasion might be slowed!

Concrete tank trap it was built
And set into the clay,
I doubt it made a difference
They'd have gone another way.

Machinery parked in farmer's field
To ward off aircraft landing,
And paratroopers if they came
Impaled on things upstanding!

A stranger in the village
Be careful what you say!
Might be a secret agent
You never know today!

Rationing in the village shop
"Sorry no more meat".
"Not even half a sausage?"
"Well, I've got some old pigs' feet!".

The village and the countryside
It wasn't quite the same,
In those war years long ago
Life was a right old game!

FILLING THE NATION'S PANTRY

Before the war we did import
Near all that we did need,
But when the U-boats blocked the route
We needed much more feed!

Every little piece of land
Was put beneath the plough,
Farming had to make a change
It really did and how!

New seeds and crops were introduced
And tractor did appear,
Production had to be stepped up
Starvation was the fear!

I guess it was the start of all
The modern farming way,
There was no other option
And it really saved the day!

THE LAND ARMY

When war broke out in '39
To the farms the ladies went,
There was a need for labour
And so their backs they bent.

The government formed an army
But armed them not with guns,
Instead they fought with horse and plough
Producing food in tons.

Like any other soldiers
A uniform they wore,
Breeches, boots and overalls
The cut was rather poor!

They joined up from the cities
And from the fancy set,
Some had never seen a cow
A challenge not yet met!

Learning how to milk was hard
And hours were so long,
But as the weeks and months went by
They soon became quite strong.

Living in government hostels
They learnt to work and play,
Not always liked by village women
'Twas said they'd lead men astray!

The role they played was vital
To keep the nation fed,
Allowing men to go to war
To take up arms instead.

The author's mother in typical Land Army attire, circa 1941.

'NEATH BATTLE-TORN SKIES

The Battle of Britain raged above
While men farmed down below,
A desperate struggle, who would win?
That they did not know.

Workers stood out in the fields
And gazed up to the sky,
For sight of shot down Messerschmitt
They searched with eagle eye.

Contrails crossed the azure blue
A plane looked like a speck,
But sometimes when they came down low
Farm worker hit the deck!

German bombers shed their load
When met by British fighters,
Often sheep and cows were killed
Those rotten lousy blighters!

A parachute would drift on down
Farm worker ran to meet,
And if it was an Englishman
He'd help him to his feet.

When German plane crashed landed
Warm reception he would get,
Prodded with a pitchfork
His match he'd truly met!

Angry skies and dangerous times
Farm work carried on below,
Those days were far from easy
That you'll surely know!

The Home Guard under inspection.

THE HOME GUARD

The call went out for volunteers
To form a local guard,
And to make that mob a fighting force
Well, that was really hard!

From farm and village
They all came,
The young, the old,
Some deaf and lame!

On parade with broomsticks
Marching up and down,
Not only in the country
But also in the town.

They did their job throughout the day
Then on duty every night,
They swore that if old Hitler came
They'd put his boys to flight!

Standing guard on coastal watch
Or maybe on church tower,
They knew they had a job to do
And felt a sense of power.

If indeed invasion came
No chance for them they knew,
But stand and fight they would have done
They would have seen it through!

THE EVACUEES

When war came to the city
And bombs began to fall,
"Move the children to the country"
Was the nation's call.

Packed off at the railway station
With gas mask and suitcase,
Thousands of evacuees
Looked for a safer place.

Arriving in the villages
Lost and all alone,
Then there was a problem
To find them all a home.

One to every household
That had some room to sparc,
Brother and sister torn apart
No-one much did care.

Homesick and so lonely
No mum and dad in sight,
Many was the tear that rolled
From eyes that stared with fright.

The countryside was strange to them
So much they had not seen,
They never would have gone there
If war there had not been.

Some were treated very well
And others maybe not,
But for those wartime evacuees
The experience is not forgot!

THE PRISONERS OF WAR

Brought out to the farms in trucks
Working under guard,
They helped to bring the harvest in
Their life was not so hard!

I'm told they often worked as well
As any free Englishman,
Not often causing trouble
And escape they did not plan.

When the war was over
Many here did stay,
Married, raised a family,
And still are here today.

THE AMERICAN INVASION

They came in by the thousand
So brash and very loud,
Their uniforms were very smart
They walked around so proud.

Fields became an airbase
For bomber or a fighter,
Girls they had a'plenty
Because their smile was whiter!

Money was no problem
They really had no care,
Their rations were so plentiful
With village folk they'd share.

Jealousy raged far and wide
Folk said they're over-sexed!
They buy the favours that they get
With gifts bought from their own PX!

Either loved or hated
Not much in-between,
But one thing that is still recalled
Their spirit was not mean.

Look about the countryside
They've left their mark around,
Restoration of village church
Squadron memorial on the ground.

NATURE'S LARDER

People who lived in the countryside of my younger day were blessed with varied and bountiful supplies of food supplied by Mother Nature.

In springtime, we would walk the ditch banks, collecting the most wonderfully flavoured eggs from the moorhen's nests built among the reeds. Sometimes, if the nests were in mid-stream, then a spoon fastened to a long stick would enable them to be reached. They were so plentiful in number that the possibility of diminishing the species never occurred to us.

The nests of the mallard duck were no less numerous, but were so much harder to find. It is the habit of the mallard to cover its nest with sedge before going off to feed and rarely does she fly straight from the nest, preferring instead to creep along the ditch bank for several yards before taking off. Despite the difficulties of locating duck nests, the monotony of moorhen's eggs would be broken by the occasional find of a more carelessly placed nest.

The green plover or lapwing always laid in a sparse nest flat on the ground, most usually in either a ploughed field or in between rows of winter wheat. There was an easy way to tell if the eggs contained a chick or rich yellow yolk. Depending on the state of advancement, the position of the eggs changed, starting off in the early days the narrow pointed end of the egg points away from the nest; by the later stages it has moved round to point toward the centre of the nest. If this were the case, you did not bother to pick them up, but otherwise their flavour was most acceptable.

It was hardly possible to go hungry if you lived in the countryside in those days. Many countrymen kept ferrets for rabbiting or owned a gun. Hares, pigeons and ducks would all find their way into the pot, along with the rabbit. By reading the tracks and judicious placement of a snare it was possible to dine on rabbit pie even if you owned neither gun nor ferrets.

If pheasant was upon your table it was more likely that it had been poached, as might be the case with partridge. My father was not adverse to a little poaching, though he was strictly a 'one for the pot' man.

Eels fished from a ditch, skinned and fried in the pan, have an unbelievable flavour. Pike, oven baked or fried, was also a favourite. Roach and perch tend to be rather boney and to have a rather muddy flavour and so when, as small boys fishing, we caught those, we tended to put them back.

Horse mushrooms were common place and we fed upon them until thoroughly sick of the sight. In the woodland, there were chestnuts, hazelnuts and, less common, walnuts. Wild strawberries were a special treat and wild cherries, although a little sharp, made a perfectly good pie when sweetened.

The environmental changes have destroyed the habitat of many species that were once so common place. For myself, although my memories of collecting and gathering food from the land are happy ones, these days I prefer to observe wildlife rather than to shoot or snare it.

A typical Romney Marsh dyke, from which eels were fished and the eggs of the moorhen were collected.

NATURE'S FEAST

Near a place where once I lived
There was a mighty field,
Through late summer into autumn
We fed on nature's yield.

The finest mushrooms you could find
Grew in secret places,
To find them in the morning mist
Put smiles on our faces.

To pluck them at their very best
You had to get up early,
Soaked in dew and oh so fresh
Their flesh so white and pearly.

The flavour I can't find today
From those bought in the shops,
Those wild-grown mushrooms of my yesterday
They really were the tops!

ROOK PIE

A country dish of years ago
Was pie crust over rook!
And if you want the recipe
Then look in old cook book.

Skin your rook and clean it out
The younger birds are best,
Arrange them in a pie dish
Put bacon on the breast.

Season well with salt and pepper
Add stock and dripping too,
Make sure your oven's nice and hot
Then bake for an hour or two.

I do not know of anyone
Whose eaten of rook pie,
And as for me, I do not think
That it I'll ever try!

WOODLAND TREATS

I used to love to search and hunt
For nature's little treats,
I'll tell about the things I found
Those special little 'eats'.

In autumn to the woods I'd go
Chestnuts for to find,
Later when I got back home
By fireside I dined.

Shaggy inkcup turned to soup
A flavour hard to beat,
Wild strawberries in the summertime
They tasted oh so sweet!

Jams and jellies mother made
From crabapples and blackberries,
Pies with thickest pastry crust
Deep filled with wild picked cherries.

Those woods have now been lost for good
Replaced by spruce and pine,
Those little treats I used to love
Will never again be mine.

A FRESHER FISH

Fresh fish today is quite rare
It's usually been on ice,
The flavour tends to fade away
I find it not so nice.

Years ago, a chore I had,
It happened once a week,
I would cycle to the coast
For fish I had to seek.

At Dungeness, a very small fleet
Would sell to all who bought,
If you ever go that way
To buy some you had ought.

Fillets of cod were the best,
Dover sole and plaice,
But if you wanted sprats for tea
Then you would have to race.

Sometimes on a rare event
That flavour I can find,
But even if I don't again
It's etched upon my mind.

BARNYARD FOWL

We always had Rhode Island Reds
A scratching in the yard,
It was my job to hunt for eggs
And that was sometimes hard.

There always was a dozen
And some at point of lay,
I had to feed them and collect
Before I went to play.

They used to lay in hidden places
That I do recall,
Like underneath a manger
In our old bull's stall.

A broody hen might find a nest
Some distance right away,
Then you'd see her with her chicks
After hatching day.

We had a mighty cockerel
He used to rule the yard,
One day he came up to me
And pecked me very hard!

Those eggs were full of flavour
Richness personified,
We used to have them every day
Scrambled, poached or fried.

THE UNSPOILT COUNTRYSIDE

So much is written and said today of how our British countryside has been spoilt. Planners and developers, farmers and industry, all at one time or another have been labelled as the culprits. It is true that huge swathes of our natural heritage have been changed and lost forever.

If I think of my own birthplace, Romney Marsh, one of the earliest settled parts of England, I remember a place that, thirty years ago, consisted of tiny fields interspersed with dykes and hedgerows. Laying below sea level, much of the marsh was flooded for weeks on end in wintertime. Traditionally, the marsh was the finest area in the country for sheep. When the sea receded from Romney Marsh, it left behind what became the richest pasture land.

After the second world war a change, slow at first, took place. A programme of drainage was introduced that enabled the land to be farmed in different ways. The sheep began to reduce in numbers and pastures that had never seen the plough were turned over to the production of cereals and potatoes. During the late 1960s and 1970s, farm machinery went through a revolutionary phase. Suddenly, bigger was better. More acres might be ploughed in a day and the harvest time might be reduced. Of equal consideration, fewer tractors and reduced labour came into the equation as farming moved into the most profitable phase in living memory. There was, however, a problem. Many of the traditional fields were of a non-practical size to accommodate the advances in machinery. The answer? Simple! Drain the land still further, fill in the dykes, and remove the hedgerows. Result? A new landscape. On the positive side, production costs were reduced and I have no problem with that. On the downside, wildlife habitat was destroyed and species that I knew so well as a boy became rare. Skylarks, yellow hammers - even the number of sparrows has been reduced.

If you cannot remember the way it was, then you cannot be nostalgic for what is lost. It is also true to say that, as the habitat changes, new species make an appearance, sometimes. I cannot accept that the changes were not necessary. It was Napoleon who claimed that we were a nation of shopkeepers; he was only partly right. We have been a nation of farmers from the earliest times; today, much less so than at any other time in living memory. Time and time again, we have been told to reduce our cost of production to remain competitive, never mind the fact that we produce food to a higher standard than most anywhere in the world, from where food is imported into this country! Every time that a change is brought about that just might give an advantage to cost of production, somewhere along the line there is a casualty. It will be either the visual aspect of the countryside, or a reduction in the numbers of people who are employed in rural industry.

In all of these changes, there are things that must be

remembered. If you take from the land, you must put back. If the body is taken from the land, you destroy it. In the Midwest of America, a dustbowl was created in the 1930s by poor farming. The land simply blew away. I am not suggesting that the same thing will happen here, although removing the hedgerows was a good way to start the process. The warning signs were heeded and now a hedge-planting grant is available.

I am never sure how much of our countryside has been spoilt and how much has merely been 'changed' or 'rearranged'. To me, 'spoilt' is a new quarry that rips the very guts out of the land. 'Spoilt' is a new hypermarket on a green field site, or a new housing development carelessly placed. I sometimes think that, in the minds of some, there is a belief that an optimum environment can be achieved and maintained without change. Our environment has changed continuously over thousands upon thousands of years. Every succeeding generation has mourned the loss of his past and been slow to praise the new, and so it will continue. Nothing, or very little, stays as it is forever. We do have a responsibility to ensure that each change is not to the permanent detriment of the future.

There are, however, many thousands of acres of countryside that have not changed and will not be changed for a variety of reasons. Go out and find them, see for yourself.

Fairfield on Romney Marsh.
A most unspoilt place.

FAIRFIELD

I know a place
Where the bulrush grows,
Where fat sheep graze
A tiny stream flows.

A lonely church
Stands out on its own,
Around its spire
Restless winds moan.

No village green
Nor boundary signs,
This ancient hamlet
Has no well-defined lines.

Venture along the winding lanes
Look and you will see,
Farms that stand out all alone
The stunted, wind-blown tree.

Regally poised upon ditch bank
Grey heron waits for a catch,
A silver eel glides on through
For heron he is no match.

Fairfield surely has not changed
It never has to me,
If a peaceful place you must seek
Then Fairfield holds the key.

DRY STONE WALLS

Up around the hills and dales
See the old stone wall,
Marking pasture's boundary
But many now they fall.

Laid by hand from local stone
More often not of lime,
Broken down and crumbling
They show the pass of time.

Stone of varied shape and size
Brought in by horse and cart,
Waller measured ground by eye
Flat stones he used to start.

Choosing every piece with care
Keep the layers tight,
This wall must stand for many years
So it must be laid right.

Fill in all the little gaps
Then level off the top,
Make sure the stones they interlock
And on the ground can't drop.

Built by men whose eye was true
How many of us could?
The dry stone walls must be preserved
Most certainly they should!

The dry stone waller at work.

BEAUTIFUL HEDGES

To me a hedge is a thing of beauty
But only if kept well,
I've cut and laid a hedge by hand
With pride my chest did swell.

I cannot stand to see a hedge
That's ripped and torn apart,
It sends a pain right through me
And wounds me to the heart.

A hedge is such a lovely thing
It's filled with life so good,
Hedges need to be preserved
It's clear they really should.

Hedges are a place of rest
For birds to roost and nest,
Blackthorn is a sight in spring
To me, holly is the best.

Hedges keep the land intact
And stop it blowing away,
If you think to cut your hedge
Please do it in a kindly way.

THE HEDGE LAYER'S CRAFT

A hedge so ragged and unkempt
Improvements must be made,
It's time to call the hedger in
That hedge it must be laid.

Armed with slasher, axe and hook
With leather glove on hand,
So carefully must the job be done
It must be so well planned.

Reduce the height and bring it down
Cut some sturdy poles,
Trim them up and drive them down
They'll help to fill the holes.

Take a bough and cut it through
Just enough to bend,
Bring it down and thread it through
That way the hedge you'll mend.

When you've done it should look neat
New growth will start to sprout,
You've got a better hedge now
Of that there is no doubt!

COUNTRYSIDE MATTERS

I think about the countryside
The things that have now gone,
Does it all matter that much?
Is it all so very wrong?

The things that have now gone from sight
Life that is now lost,
Does it make a difference?
Is there really that much cost?

Suppose the skylark disappeared
And was never heard again,
There are lots who've never heard one
So they would feel no pain.

What about the harvest mouse,
Today so very rare,
Were he never seen again
Who would really care?

Elm tree has been struck by blight
There's few about today,
But were they all that special?
Who can really say.

The countryside has changed so much
It really is unreal,
And does it really matter much
What is the ideal?

THE DEMISE OF THE WATER RAT

Of rat and mole we all have read
And moles there are a'plenty,
But water rat is almost gone
The streams are almost empty.

The gentleman of the river bank
These days is hard to find,
Environment has changed for worse
It's not so very kind.

Savage mink patrols the stream
Merciless to the end,
Thrives on every swimming thing
On rat he does descend.

Water rat is nearly gone
It really won't be long,
Soon he will be remembered only
In book or maybe song.

OF GEESE AND OTHER THINGS

I've seen geese fly
On moonlit nights
And heard their distant call;
I've seen the eagle
Way up high
And that's not nearly all.

I've seen the badger
Late at night
Out for his evening stroll;
I've seen a frog
Caught by a snake
And even swallowed whole.

I've heard the barn owl
Shriek and scream
And seen him hunt at night;
I've seen the deer
Graze on the dawn
And I have seen them fight.

I've seen so much
And things of wonder
Gifts that nature brings;
But most of all
I will recall
How the tiny skylark sings.

THE MARSH REVISITED

I went down to the Marsh
Where I grew up
On a cold November day;
I visited places
That I knew
Where once I stooped to play.

The old village school
Still looks the same
It hasn't changed to see;
I looked at the house
Where I was born
It meant not much to me.

The fields that I used to know
Have changed so much,
The hedgerows have all gone;
Cold air was still
And not a sound
Where once there was bird-song.

Dungeness was still the same
A lonely barren waste.
Shingle crunched beneath my feet
As I strode along the beach;
The waves rolled in and out again
An endless rhythmic beat.

Fairfield church stands all alone
Out 'cross muddy fields;
No Sunday sermon heard these days
Its doors have long since closed.
Pale Winter sun was sinking fast
The church caught in its rays.

The sun sank fast as night came on
It was time to hit the road;
I left the Marsh so far behind
As I travelled toward home.
Nostalgic, yes, the day had been
For I am the 'look-back' kind.

IN THE AGE OF CONVERSION

Many of the traditional farm buildings that were still used for their intended purpose when I was a boy are either now derelict or have been converted into a place of sumptuous residence. The ubiquitous barn conversion needs no introduction, but what of the others?

A splendid old granary that I know is now the country home of a man who works and lives in the city from Monday to Friday. More surprisingly, cow byres that once formed part of a stockyard where father used to thatch stacks, have also fallen under the architect's spell. Perhaps the most unique of all are the oast houses. Unique because the former kiln room gives the prospect of circular accommodation.

Along with farm buildings, village railway stations, watermills and the blacksmith's shop have all found a new lease of life. It is hard to imagine that there will be public outcry if the characterless but thoroughly functional farm buildings of today are eventually allowed to fall into a state of ruin. I am equally certain that there would have been much bemusement a hundred years ago at the suggestion that anyone might actually want to live in barn or a cow byre!

THE BARNS OF YESTERDAY

Deserted barn stands all alone
Out 'cross yonder field,
Roof has fallen long ago
The doors to touch won't yield.

Crumbled walls covered in moss
Broken slates lay all around,
Entrance barred by sunken doors
It used to be so sound.

So long ago when barn was built
It was so warm inside,
Packed to the rafters, filled with hay
Where lovers used to hide.

The barns of yesterday I knew
But they are rare today,
In barns like this when I was young
On rainy days I'd play.

Modern barns are something else
No character to say,
They will not stir thoughts in me
As barns of yesterday.

A wonderful example of a Cotswold stone barn, soon to be converted.

A ROUND ROOM ON THE END

In this day of barn conversion
I know of another kind,
Down in Kent where I grew up
The oast house you will find.

A kiln you'd find in an oast
For drying of hop flower,
The roof was kind of conical
A sort of chimney tower.

Square of build but with that tower
For conversion it was ripe,
In this day of preservation
The oast's a unique type.

A unique and sought after dwelling.

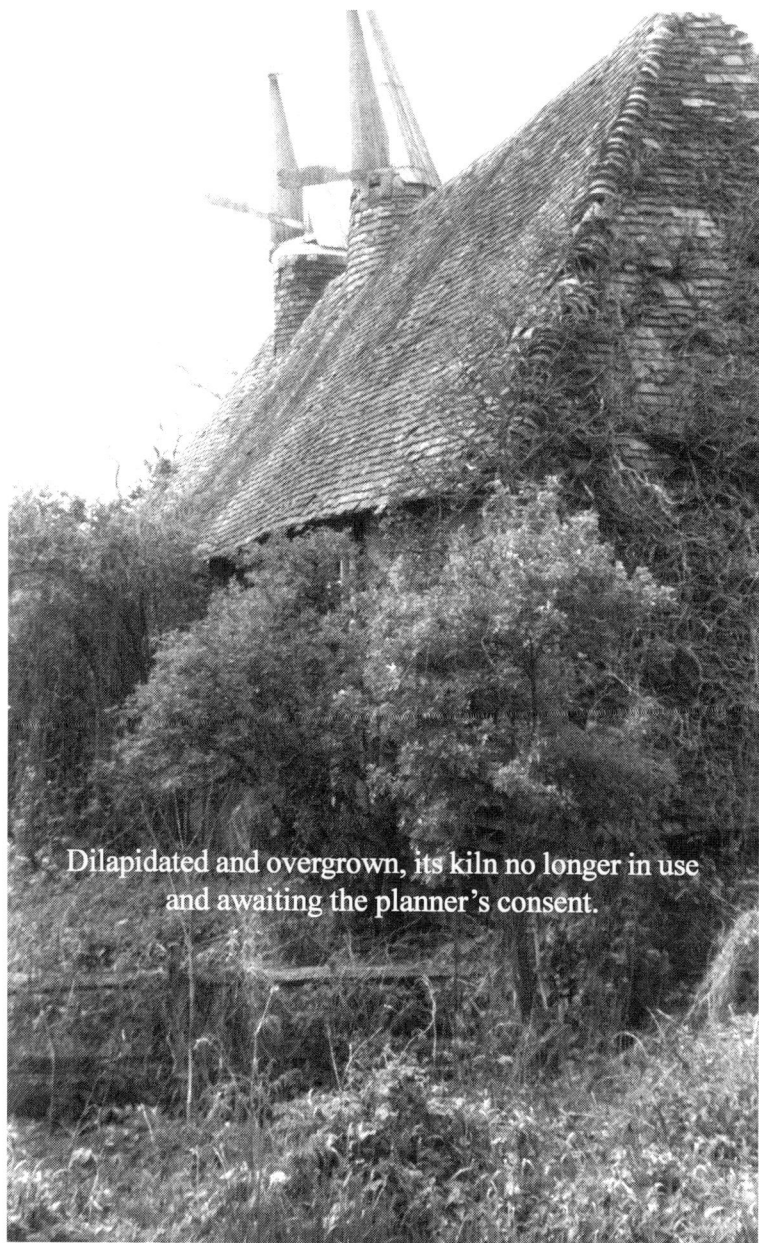

Dilapidated and overgrown, its kiln no longer in use
and awaiting the planner's consent.

OTHER FRAGMENTS REMEMBERED

There are so many memories that I have of things that are not of great significance, but none the less are stored.

As a child, I remember the sounds that would come to me as I lay a'bed on summer evenings. The distant moan of the very last steam trains as they passed a mile or so away, is one sound that I shall never forget. One hot summer night, the sound of the steam whistle came to us over and over again, there seemed to be a kind of urgency to it. The next day we heard of a terrible accident. A local man had got his tractor stuck on the tracks, trying to cross to another field. Frozen by fear, he had stayed aboard his tractor up until the very end.

The dykes where we lived were inhabited by a species of frog known as the marsh frog, although originally *rana ridibunda* came from central Europe. It was introduced to Romney Marsh in 1935 and quickly spread throughout. The Latin name *ridibunda* means 'laughing', and that is the sound that this rather large frog makes. On summer nights, the racket that these creatures made could literally keep you awake. Due to mass drainage and the loss of ditches and dykes, *ridibunda* is far less common, but can still be heard.

In winter, I loved to listen to the screech and hoot of owls. They would perch in the surrounding trees, or hover, waiting for some unsuspecting creature. I could mimic their call sufficiently that they would answer.

I suppose that every generation has listened to their elders proclaiming of how life was so much better in the old days. I have listened and thought and ruminated over this one, long and hard. My mother tells of village children struck down by diphtheria; old men coughing blood discreetly into handkerchiefs; polio and the like. Certainly, we are in better health today. We do not tend to go hungry either. One day during the early 1930s, my mother witnessed something that you would not be likely to see today. On her way to school, along with a small group of other children, a crust of bread was spotted in a puddle. A fight ensued between two hungry lads for the questionable pleasure of what was probably an unexpected breakfast! Both of my maternal great-grandparents had died of 'natural causes' before they were sixty. No executive stress, but impoverishment, health care that had to be paid for on the spot and only the poorhouse to look forward to if you were out of work.

The lot of the housewife must surely be easier today. I remember my mother doing the family washing by hand and praying for a drying wind. Convenience foods? None; there were good wholesome meals with vegetables grown in the garden, but it was a time-consuming chore. No vacuum cleaner, only a mop, scrubbing brush and sore knees! Ah yes, life moved at a slower pace, but you were old before your time.

I have my father's old shoe last. It is an iron contraption that will last forever. I can just remember him mending his work boots on it but I am glad that I never had to have my shoes mended for I have heard stories to make your hair curl! My grandmother was in seventh heaven if she found an old tyre. Roughly cut and tacked on with whatever nails she could find, many was the time my mother would discover a nail coming up through the inner sole of her shoe!

Like many, I have sometimes fallen into the trap of thinking, "Oh, I wish I'd lived in those days!". Indeed, some things may have been better, but on balance I am not convinced. It makes no difference, for we have what we have today and must make the very most of it, and make sure that when our time is through, we have lived our life to the best of our ability.

A GOLDEN AGE

Olden times were better
They say
A time when children
Could safely play.

No pollution or drugs
Nor streetwise thugs,
More to life
Was there really
Less strife?

Life did move
At a much slower pace
Who'd ever heard of
The term 'Rat Race'?

No welfare state
or National Health,
Bellies often empty
And sickness a'plenty.

Out of work
The poorhouse beckoned,
No first chance given
Let alone a second.

From 'fourteen to 'eighteen
War did rage,
Conscription took men
Of a certain age.

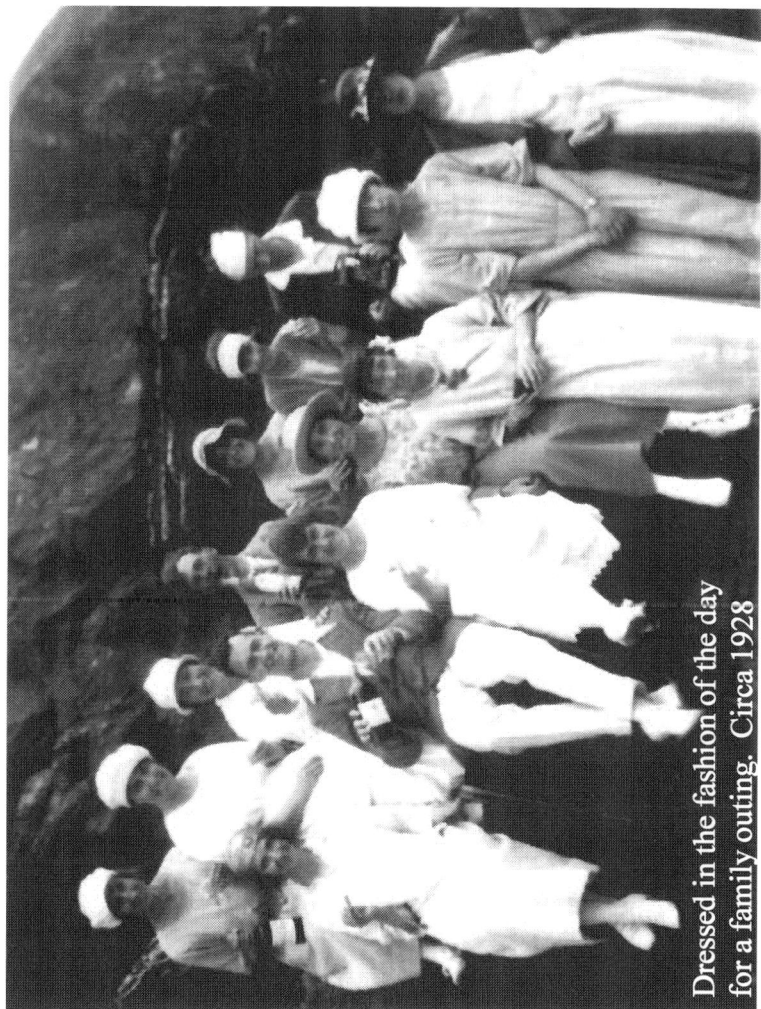

Dressed in the fashion of the day for a family outing. Circa 1928

Every family felt
The Grim Reaper's hand
Lost their sons
In a foreign land.

Look back today
It's easy to say
'That was a time'
'Those were the days'.
But were they much better?
Who can remember . . .
Detail to the letter?

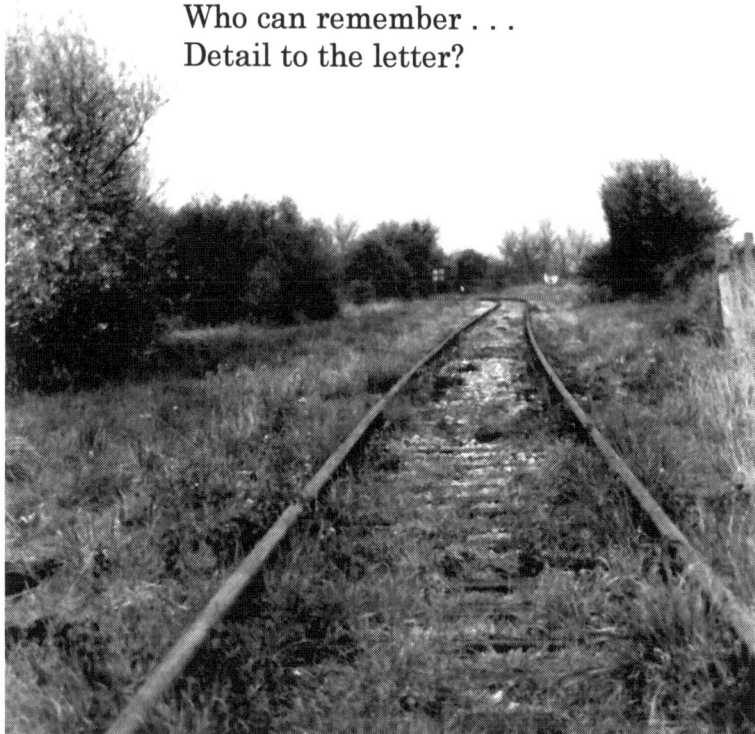

As a small boy, I remember the last of the steam trains
thundering down this track.
Now weed infested and unusued.

NIGHT SOUNDS IN THE COUNTRY

A barking fox not far away
It always sounded eerie,
I would lay a'bed at night
And listen 'til I was weary.

Tawny owl would hoot and hiss
Barn owl it would scream,
Sometimes when I was asleep
The sound would break my dream.

Croaking frogs in summer
Would echo all night long,
For such a tiny creature
Their call it was so strong.

Sheep moved to new pasture
Their lambs they could not find,
They'd bleat and moan for hours
That really was a bind!

Steam train in the distance
Made a mournful sound,
Always sounded weary
As it thundered over ground.

Cockerel crowing early dawn
Why can't he just sleep on?
Those night-time sounds of years ago
Some of them have gone.

DAYS OF STEAM

An anorak or woolly hat
I have never had,
I've never been a trainspotter
Of that I am quite glad.

I do though like to see the sight
Of a steam train chuffing by,
The mournful sound its whistle makes
And clouds of smoke that billow high.

The last days of steam I do recall
I lived quite near the tracks,
Now steam has gone and diesel rules
The sound it something lacks.

I'd stand and watch when I was small
Those monsters thunder by,
The ground beneath my feet would shake
In Summer dust would fly.

Late at night I'd lay a'bed
And hear that whistle moan,
It always seemed to sound to me
A lost and lonely tone.

There's something quite poetic
About an old steam train,
But what about a diesel?
I think I will refrain!

The Romney, Hythe and Dymchurch railway.
Still operating today.

THE COUNTRY WIFE

Strong of limb she had to be
And tremendously resourceful,
No time to sit and watch TV
Nor even to be thoughtful!

Up at early hours
To get breakfast for her man,
Not orange juice and muesli
But bacon in the pan!

Black-leading grate and scrubbing floors
Down on hands and knees,
Time to get the dinner on
Dig spuds and pick some peas.

Churning butter and baking bread
"I've got the washing done,
But at the end of every day
I'll never feel I've won!".

The life was often lonely
Much more so than today,
How many housewives do you know
Would want a life that way?

WASH DAY BLUES

Water boiled in brick built copper
Fire down below,
Washing was a dreary job
It was so very slow.

Everything was done by hand
Scrubbed on an old wash board,
Hands were always red and raw
Of that you can be assured.

Rinsed in water oh so cold
Then squeezed out through a mangle,
Those wooden rollers did their best
But it was a right old fangle.

No tumble dryer in those days
Facilities were lacking,
Sunlight, soap and whipping wind
Meant towels that felt like sacking.

It must have taken near all day
The washing for to do,
To wash the clothes by hand today
Would make you feel so blue!

COUNTRY COOKING

As country folk we ate so well
Our variety was wide,
Rabbit, hare or pigeon
Stewed, casseroled or pied.

Pheasant roast with bacon fat
A flavour oh so rich,
But a treat that I most enjoyed
Was fried eels caught from a ditch.

Fruit and veg we grew our own
Carrots, spuds and greens,
I've never had the like again
Of father's runner beans!

In this day of processed food
Deep freeze and microwave,
We've said 'goodbye' to flavour
For ease is what we crave.

THE FAMILY SHOE LAST

Every family had a last
Shoes and boots for mending,
Footwear had to be repaired
For there was little cash for spending.

A lump of iron that it was
With feet of different sizes,
Repairs were often not so neat
And would not win no prizes!

A cast-off tyre was a find
Something you could use,
Cut and nailed upon the last
To sole the children's shoes.

Walking on the way to school
Father's used long nails,
If they came up through the sole
Then you would hear some wails!

The families' shoes of years ago
Were mended on a last,
You'll find them in a junk shop
They're confined now to the past!

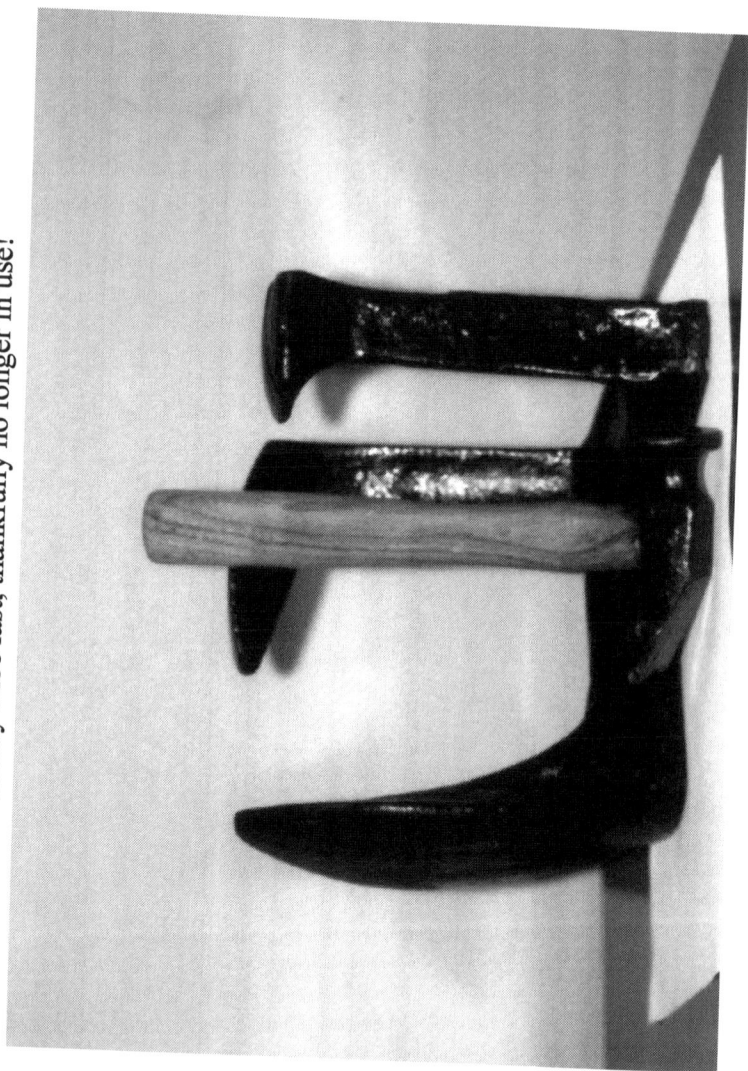

The family shoe last, thankfully no longer in use!

HOB NAIL BOOTS

I yearned for real boots
When I was a lad,
I wanted to walk
Just like my dad.

I loved the sound
Of nailed soles on the road,
That clickety clack
Was like a musical ode.

I saved up my pennies
From chores I had done,
Got me some boots
But they weighed a ton!

When I wore those boots
I felt ever so proud,
Folk heard me coming
I walked oh so loud.

Many are the pairs
I've had since then,
But that first pair
I remember now and then.